JANG

JANG

The Soul of Korean Cooking

MINGOO KANG

with
Joshua David Stein and Nadia Cho

ARTISAN
NEW YORK

Library of Congress Cataloging-in-Publication Data

Names: Kang, Mingoo, author. | Stein, Joshua David, author. | Cho, Nadia, author.
Title: Jang : the soul of Korean cooking / Mingoo Kang with Joshua David Stein
    and Nadia Cho.
Description: New York, NY : Artisan, [2024] | Includes index.
Identifiers: LCCN 2023033565 | ISBN 9781648291869 (hardback)
Subjects: LCSH: Cooking, Korean. | Hot pepper sauces—Korea. | Fermented
    soyfoods—Korea. | Cooking (Fermented foods) | LCGFT: Cookbooks.
Classification: LCC TX360.K6 K37 2024 | DDC 641.59519—dc23/eng/20230724
LC record available at https://lccn.loc.gov/2023033565

Design by Suet Chong
Cover design by Suet Chong
Cover photographs by Dong-gil Yun

Artisan books may be purchased in bulk for business, educational, or promotional
use. For information, please contact your local bookseller or the Hachette Book
Group Special Markets Department at special.markets@hbgusa.com.

The publisher is not responsible for websites (or their content) that are not
owned by the publisher.

The Hachette Speakers Bureau provides a wide range of authors for speaking
events. To find out more, go to hachettespeakersbureau.com or email
HachetteSpeakers@hbgusa.com.

Published by Artisan,
an imprint of Workman Publishing,
a division of Hachette Book Group, Inc.
1290 Avenue of the Americas
New York, NY 10104
artisanbooks.com

The Artisan name and logo are registered trademarks of Hachette Book Group, Inc.

Printed in China on responsibly sourced paper

First printing, February 2024

10 9 8 7 6 5 4 3 2 1

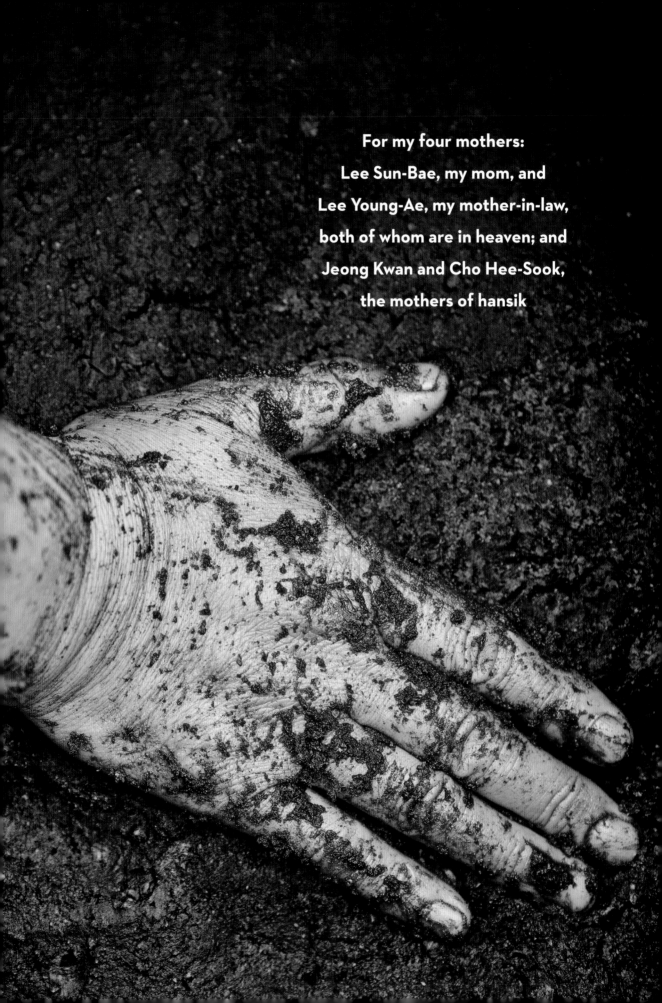

For my four mothers:
Lee Sun-Bae, my mom, and
Lee Young-Ae, my mother-in-law,
both of whom are in heaven; and
Jeong Kwan and Cho Hee-Sook,
the mothers of hansik

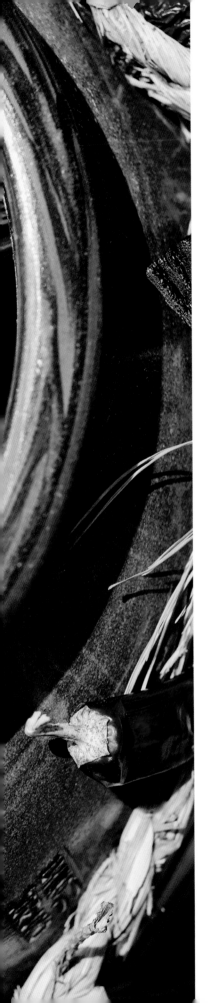

CONTENTS

FOREWORD

by Eric Ripert

I have had the good fortune to travel to South Korea numerous times. I've experienced the energetic and vibrant lifestyle of Seoul and the beautiful and peaceful countryside of the peninsula. In my travels, I have always felt my hosts' warmth and excitement to share their culture with me.

On my first visit, I was fascinated and overwhelmed by the difference between the food culture of my world—the West— and what Seoul offered through a multitude of restaurants, bars, and food stands. I was most impressed by the bansang, the traditional way of serving Korean cuisine in which all the different ingredients and condiments are presented at the table at once. The flavors were not very familiar to me, nor was this way of eating, so different from the linear Western style. But such an array led to an interesting and convivial experience with the rest of the guests.

I quickly came to understand that Korean cuisine is not shy about using strong and pungent ingredients, such as kimchi and aekjeot, to elevate the meal to another level. But I sensed that there was something much deeper going on, too. At first I couldn't identify what it was. Then I visited artisanal factories in the countryside dedicated to crafting gochujang, doenjang, and ganjang, and the secret was unlocked. I tasted the jangs while witnessing the process and even participating in the making of these key fermented sauces. I observed with much respect the ancient tradition of creating something very special with just three ingredients: soybeans, water, and salt. I started to understand the importance and impact of temperature, weather conditions, time, fermentation, and how these details come together to make the perfect jang. Jang is the result of a magical alchemy between the effects of nature and human interaction. It had been the flavor I couldn't quite place that underscored so much of what I enjoyed at the table.

Food can be powerful medicine, and it is important to cook with knowledge and love. Today, I realize that I still have so much to learn. I am grateful to all my teachers, seculars and monastics, and to Chef Mingoo Kang for this much-needed book. Thank you for sharing with us essential ingredients that define not just Korean cuisine but much more: an entire special and beautiful culture. With this book, we all pay homage to an ingredient that says it all: jang!

INTRODUCTION

Imagine trying to understand Italian cooking without olive oil or to unlock French cuisine without butter and cream. It would be impossible. The same is true of jang (which rhymes with "song") when it comes to Korean cuisine. I think hansik, or Korean cooking, is one of the most intriguing and dynamic of the world's culinary traditions. (I am biased, but also correct.) That the entirety of Korean cuisine relies on what is to most people a near secret ingredient is one of the last great discoveries in world cookery.

Many factors have contributed to jang being virtually unheard of outside Korean kitchens; none of them has to do with the characteristics or quality or potency of jang itself. That's why I'm so excited to expose the world to the deep history, expressive power, and vibrant flavors of jang. In doing so, I hope to not only shine a spotlight on this wonderful family of ingredients but also open a gateway to a deeper understanding of Korean cuisine and culture itself—much as the extra-virgin olive oil boom of the 1990s increased the popularity of regional Italian cooking or, more recently, a growing appreciation of za'atar and tahini, among other such ingredients, underwrote the explosion of interest in Middle Eastern cooking.

So what are jangs? On one hand, jangs are deceptively simple. The word *jang* (장) means "fermented soybean paste." There are three main types of jang: gochujang, doenjang, and ganjang. Gochujang is a fiery fermented chile paste, perhaps the best known beyond the Korean peninsula; doenjang is a thick fermented soybean paste; and ganjang is a thin, dark liquid. For doenjang and ganjang, analogs exist in the form of Japanese miso and shoyu soy sauce, respectively. For gochujang, which is derived from Korea's endemic gochu chile, there is really no comparison. Yet I would argue that all three Korean sauces are utterly unique.

Like that of charcuterie, cheese, or wine, the character of jang is determined by time and place, and, of course, great human skill. The three types of jang are deeply interconnected, though ultimately, their paths diverge. Jang itself is a buttress against waste, and so it makes sense that nothing in the process is wasteful. Methods vary from producer to producer: Where the jang is fermented and for how long and under what conditions and with what additives, as well as how warm the summer or cold the winter and dozens of other factors, all contribute to the infinite variability and complexity of jang.

All three start in the fields when, in the late autumn, farmers harvest soybeans across the Korean countryside. The soybeans are dried and sold to jang makers—and others—who boil them down into a paste. This paste is then compressed into blocks called meju, which are wrapped in rice stalk straws and hung to air-cure. In December or January, depending on the ambient conditions, the blocks are transferred to large earthen vessels called jangdok (also known as onggi), which are placed outside directly upon the earth. At this point, some of the meju is ground into a powder, which is then mixed with gochugaru (ground dried Korean red chiles), salt, glutinous rice powder, and a few other ingredients and placed in its own jangdok. This, eventually, becomes gochujang.

To make ganjang and doenjang, salted water is added to the blocks of meju in the jangdok and they are left to ferment. After some period of time, usually between sixty and ninety days, the fermented soybean mixture is mashed and strained. The liquid, which is aged longer in its own vessel, becomes ganjang. The solids, which are aged further in their own container, become doenjang.

These liquids, in the case of ganjang, and pastes, in the case of doenjang and gochujang, are not simply fermented soybeans but really the result of thousands of years of tradition, generations of experience, and a million small decisions made by jang artisans. Jangs are employed everywhere in Korean cuisine, from soups and stews to salads and marinades and even in desserts. They are the very marrow of my country's cooking.

FINDING HANSIK

I have to admit, I was a latecomer to the magic of jang. Born and raised in Seoul, I've wanted to be a chef for as long as I can remember. Though my mother was a decent home cook—my father, like many Korean men, did not cook at home—I fell in love with cooking like many kids do, by sitting in front of the television. Watching food and travel documentaries, I used to

dream of running a kitchen of my own. As soon as I could, I
started studying hospitality and culinary arts in Seoul; I took
advantage of my mandatory military service to serve as a chef
for a navy admiral. Fresh out of the navy and hungry for adventure
and experience, I set out for the United States, where I found a
job at Nobu Matsuhisa's eponymous restaurant in Miami. Thus
began a culinary path that took me to the Bahamas and to the
Basque Country. Like many in the Korean diaspora, whether
I was cooking Matsuhisa's refined Japanese cuisine or Martín
Berasategui's avant-garde preparations, I missed hansik, the
flavors of my home. So I returned to Korea to try my hand at a
place of my own.

When I opened Mingles in 2014, my mission was to meld—or
mingle—Western and Korean traditions. At the time, Korean fine
dining really meant Korean chefs cooking Italian or French haute
cuisine. Korean chefs cooking Korean food merited hardly any
attention. What we were doing at Mingles was unique. Though I
obviously incorporated elements and techniques from my years
abroad, the heart of the cuisine was all hansik. Like Massimo
Bottura or René Redzepi before me, I was adamant about uplifting
my own country's ingredients, techniques, and traditions,
proving that hansik belonged in the pantheon of the world's great
cuisines. The acclaim was immediate, and so was the pressure. I
felt a responsibility to truly educate myself in Korean cuisine and
ingredients in a more formal way than I had.

This quest brought me to the feet of two of Korea's food gods:
Cho Hee-Sook, who was later named Asia's Best Female Chef, and
the Buddhist nun Jeong Kwan, made famous through her episode
of the Netflix series *Chef's Table*. In culinary terms, Cho is like
Paul Bocuse, and Jeong Kwan, even though she is not technically
a chef, is an analog to Alain Ducasse and Joël Robuchon. Cho's

humble (and humbling) classes returned me to the rich simplicity of hansik. It was Chef Cho who introduced me to the ability of jang, especially ganjang, to replace salt in most of my cooking. But it was a visit to Jeong Kwan's monastery that changed my life.

By the time I walked through the wooden gates of the ancient grounds of Baekyangsa, a Buddhist temple at the foot of Naejang Mountain on the southern tip of the peninsula, I had been cooking Korean food for nearly twenty years. Mingles had been open for three years, and though we were busy, I was at a crossroads. For better or worse, I had come to represent modern hansik to the parade of foreign chefs who stopped in Seoul. And yet I felt there was something missing in my understanding of hansik. I had a feeling I might find the answer at Baekyangsa.

The grounds were about as far from the fast-paced world of the professional kitchen as could be, and quiet, until I eventually learned to listen for the birdsong and the rustle of grass. Stands of yew trees formed tunnels for twisted footpaths that led to peaceful open spaces with altars holding golden statues of Buddha. Stones set into the ground hundreds of years ago by monks long past were covered in moss. I had come on a pilgrimage to learn the essence of Korean cuisine from Jeong Kwan, a Buddhist nun who ran away from home at the age of seventeen to join the order and had been cooking for her fellow practitioners at the temple ever since. Her style of extremely simple, extremely vibrant sachal eumsik (temple cuisine) has made her famous throughout Korea. I yearned to meet her, and after some petitioning, I had my chance. I didn't know it as I mounted the steps for our first encounter, but I was also beginning my journey to jang.

No Korean can be wholly ignorant of jang. From my earliest food memories, jangs had been present at nearly all my meals. Doenjang contributed the depth of flavor and rich backbone of the soups and stews my mother made me after school. Ganjang served as an umami-rich marinade for fish, a steaming liquid for vegetables, and a light broth for soups. Gochujang added a kick of heat to everything from pork to seafood to bibimbap. But as surrounded by it as I was, and even as I had progressed through the stages of culinary training, first in Seoul and then abroad, I had always thought of jang as just another ingredient: useful, of course, but nothing out of the ordinary. As is true for many Koreans, the jangs I used were industrial products, manufactured in large facilities by companies like Chung Jung One and Sempio. And if I couldn't find ganjang, what was the harm in substituting Japanese shoyu instead? The same could be said for doenjang and the tubs of miso I could buy from the restaurant depot on the outskirts of Seoul. Such was my thinking when I first saw the petite shaven head of Jeong Kwan, a sixty-something-year-old woman, sticking up out of the folds of her robes as she approached me. She bowed, I bowed, and she led me toward the monastery kitchen.

As I watched her, I marveled that Jeong Kwan didn't cook so much as simply let the earth move through her. I followed her as she wandered through the temple garden, plucking a head of cabbage or pulling turnips from the ground. We clambered up the steep mountain behind the monastery, hunting pyogo (shiitake) mushrooms, which she carefully placed in her wicker basket. Then we made our way to the kitchen, as clean and airy as a meditation hall.

Using the few ingredients we had gathered, she produced a simple meal that seemed to have only a hair's-breadth separation from the land itself. How? Soon I realized the answer: jang. Jangs were omnipresent in her work. This was, perhaps, not unexpected, but I was intrigued by the small unlabeled terra-cotta pots laid out just outside the kitchen in a sun-kissed courtyard, and then surprised when she told me they all held jangs of various ages. She told me how each jang had its own individual character, its own story, its own spirit. A combination of factors—time, place, the angle at which the breeze swept in from the sea or the pattern of shade cast by stands of bamboo and pine trees—affected the complicated patina of flavors of the substance inside. I could taste how the same jang, aged three, five, or ten years, matured, mellowed, and revealed its depth and complexity as it grew. It reminded me of tasting through glasses of extraordinary wine or whiskey. This was my moment of awakening.

These jangs were alive, each tingling with its own expression. Mixtures of only soybean, water, and salt—and sometimes a few aromatics—the jangs relied on their environment and subtle

human intervention to develop. Though certainly the fields in which the soybeans were grown played a part, so much of a jang's character depends on how and where it is allowed to ferment. The air, the wind, the biome are indelibly etched into flavor. A jang from Jeju Island in the middle of the Southern Sea of Korea, for instance, is more intensely flavorful and bitter than the famously gentle jangs from Paju, in the north.

Like all fermented products, jangs rely on the interactions between bacteria and sugar as expressed through time. As with all naturally fermented products, from sourdough to wine to lambics, these naturally occurring bacteria vary by location, according to the natural biome. Cooked, then dried and aged, and then fermented up to ten years and sometimes even longer, jangs are a true expression of terroir. In Jeong Kwan's hands, each was a string to be plucked in concert with her ingredients, a note to be played in harmony. So deep was her knowledge, so intimate was she with the characteristics of each jar, that she always knew exactly which jang to deploy and when.

EXPLORING JANG

I returned to the kitchen of Mingles with my hair on fire. I felt like I had been playing the piano by hitting only the middle C, and now the entire keyboard had been opened to me. I started seeking out and sampling artisanal jangs from across the peninsula. I began vertical tastings, in which I'd use the same jang from different years to better understand how the flavors evolved. As often as I could, I visited small producers in the foothills and forests, on mountainsides and near beaches. I got to know the mostly female artisans who tend to their jangdok year-round, wiping snow from their covers in winter, brushing bugs away in summer. I returned to learn from Jeong Kwan again and again, making the three-hour journey to her temple from Seoul on a weekly basis. As I delved deeper into the process, my appreciation for jang blossomed even more. Since opening Mingles, I had been on a mission to express the true nature of Korean cuisine. I had finally found it, and the answer had literally been in my backyard the entire time.

As these jangs began to express themselves in my cooking, I found I could do less, add less, intervene less. My approach began to shift away from the Western notion of addition and toward a more Korean one—or, more precisely, a Buddhist one—of subtraction. What step could I remove? What ingredient could I omit? When I relied on jangs, my culinary intervention (and ego) was not as needed as I thought it was. But I've also found that like any subtle tool, jangs aren't rigid; they reward experimentation. Much like Korean culture itself, they are able to assimilate and adapt to foreign concepts. I've found jangs especially suited to pairing with Italian ingredients like balsamic vinegar, olive oil, and Parmesan, all of which can similarly express their sense of place. Gochujang has the right amount of intensity to complement the muscular flavors familiar to the American palate. And ganjang, in particular, loves to play counterpoint to caramel and dairy. Just as jangs themselves evolve with time, so too has my appreciation of them.

Today much of what I do in the kitchen at Mingles begins with finding the right way to use a jang to showcase and support the other ingredients in a dish. The whole is always greater than the sum of its parts. Few of the recipes in this book, however, are drawn directly from the menu at Mingles. Most are versions of dishes I make at home for my family and friends. My appreciation for jang, naturally, has spilled over into home cooking, since the home kitchen, for thousands of years, has been the natural domain of jang. I know that for me, the latent love of jang has immeasurably enriched how I cook, taste, and appreciate food, and I hope this book—a love letter of sorts to jang—does the same for you.

THE HISTORY OF JANG

Together with my wife, Doehee; my seven-year-old son, Yunhoo; my nine-year-old daughter, Dain; and more than nine million other souls—nearly a fifth of Korea's population—I live in Seoul, a shimmering city of towering skyscrapers rushing headlong in a blur of movement. But despite the glittering stores of the Gangnam district with their endless parade of Lamborghinis and Ferraris outside, and the constant urban dynamism that churns old buildings into new ones, Korea has only recently come into the modern age. After a brutal Japanese occupation that stretched from 1910 to 1945, followed by the 6-2-5 War (what Americans call the Korean War), we emerged in 1953 an impoverished, damaged, largely rural nation, one that had advanced little over the previous hundred years.

The poverty of the Korean people, outside the rather opulent but very small demimonde of the dynastic courts, permeated every aspect of their lives. Food was no exception. The Korean diet was largely devoid of meat. A dead animal might be delicious, but a live one was more useful. (Seafood, of course, was an exception, as there is no such thing as a working fish.) As for protein, we relied on plants, some cultivated but many foraged. Even today, during spring, we hunt Japanese angelica shoots and mugwort like Italians do truffles. Rice was our staple grain, as it is across Asia, but the topography of Korea, where less than a quarter of the land is arable, means even rice was rare and precious.

Soybeans, first introduced to the peninsula from Manchuria over four thousand years ago, were our lifeline. Rich in protein and able to thrive in poor soil, soybeans sustained us. Korean cooks endeavored to unlock the life-supporting protein contained in soy with an ingenuity I find astonishing even today, using the plant to make foods that included dubu (tofu), soybean milk, soybean oil, and bean sprouts. But among all the ways of enjoying soybeans, jang is the most profound.

Koreans have been making jang in one form or another since the Three Kingdoms period, which stretched from 57 BCE to 668 CE. Murals depicting jangdok, the large earthenware vessels used to make jang, have been found in tombs dating back to the fourth century BCE. When King Sinmun, the seventh-century ruler of the Silla dynasty, married, jang was listed as part of his bride's dowry, along with liquor, rice, and dried fish. In the eleventh century, when the Khitan people of neighboring Manchuria invaded the Korean Peninsula, the Korean king distributed jang to keep his people nourished.

To me, jang embodies the ability of generations upon generations to survive and, indeed, thrive in the face of enormous challenges. Jang takes three simple ingredients—soybeans, salt, and water—and transforms them into a nutritionally dense, deeply flavorful, extremely versatile tool. For a citizenry that up until only about fifty years ago could ill afford meat and generally eschewed dairy, jang was a lifeline of protein, vitamins such as B_{12}, fiber, and many other nutrients. Today, as the Western diet has seeped into Korean culture, jangs form an important health bulwark against the overconsumption of meat and its many accompanying maladies.

Though jang might have had its roots in necessity, something wonderfully fortuitous has become clear, too: Not only are jangs delicious; they also contain a host of beneficial and salutary characteristics. Recent research has shown that doenjang contains antidiabetic, anticancer, and anti-inflammatory properties. Unsurprisingly, ganjang is similarly beneficial, and multiple studies have found it also inhibits colitis. Gochujang, like the highest level of service at a car wash, includes all these benefits *and* has proven effective in combating obesity, thanks to the capsaicin it contains.

Historically, jang was not something one bought but rather something one made. Even today, though on a much smaller scale than in the past, you'll find jangdok in backyards across the country, under the shade of red pines in mountain towns, in the windblown shanties of the Haenyeo by the coast, on patios and balconies in the major cities. In this way, jang is more like sourdough than it is like wine: Anyone can nourish a starter, but few can sustain a vineyard.

In a Confucian society like Korea's, class hierarchy—and hierarchy in general—is almost an obsession, but jang cut across social strata. In rural homes, grandmothers made modest rustic jangs, while the emperors of the Joseon dynasty zealously protected their court's jangs. The jang-go-mama, the keeper of the jangs, often a man, was an important position in the court. In well-off families, the task of making the jangs, however, fell to the eldest

female in the household. Buddhist monks, doctrinally forbidden to eat meat, perfected jang in their monasteries. No matter where one fell in society, though, the making and maintaining of jang was an important job. As the saying goes, "If the jang changes flavor, the family is in trouble."

One might think that an ingredient as common and deeply rooted in Korean culture as jang would be widely revered and broadly understood as precious, certainly within Korea, and ideally throughout the world. After all, kimchi, another fermented Korean staple, has gained iconic global status, and kimjang, the making and sharing of kimchi, was named a UNESCO Intangible Cultural Heritage in 2013. But jang has received little attention. Why?

First, starting with the Japanese occupation of Korea in 1910, the tradition of homemade jang began to decline. This coincided with the end of the six-hundred-year rule of the Confucian-influenced Joseon dynasty, a regime that privileged tradition and family units, two key components to jang making. As part of an overall brutal policy of suppressing Korean national identity, jang making at home was discouraged. Instead, Japan rapaciously siphoned off most of Korea's soybean production for Japanese use, and, in its mania for industrialization, simultaneously encouraged the establishment of jang factories.

Jang making continued to decline, hastened by famine and war, through World War II until the end of the 6-2-5 War in 1953, at which time Korea began its superfueled expansion into the modern capitalist world, a movement that almost, but not quite, signaled the end of jang culture. With so many Koreans having perished and those who survived beset by poverty and pressed for time, jang making was largely surrendered to industrial producers.

It's human nature to not prize a thing until it's extinct, as in the case of the Asian wild wolf, or endangered, as in the case of the Amur leopard—and jang. Beginning in the 2000s, the demand for artisanal jang among those who remembered it from their childhoods grew. In response, and perhaps driven by the same desire, the children of artisanal jang makers began returning to their family businesses just as their mothers (or mothers-in-law) began to grow weary of the constant attention jang demands. For the most part, this new breed of jang makers are career changers who bring fresh eyes to the ancient process. Much like the revolution in natural wine in Italy, hastened by the exodus from the city of second- and third-generation winemakers

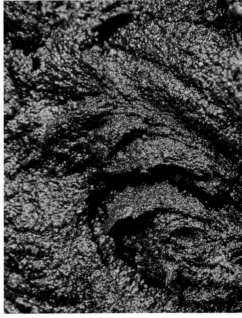

back to their family estates, this influx has reinvigorated jang production.

Simultaneously and reinforcing this, we Koreans, who have a habit of requiring external validation of our own culture, finally began receiving it. Thus, in our own eyes, Korean culture, most notably music and food, only began to seem worthy of attention domestically after it had been ratified by global culture. Today, anything with the letter *K* before it—K-pop, K-beauty, K-BBQ—is endowed with a preternatural cool. This isn't by accident. Starting in 2007, the South Korean government actively began a campaign to popularize Korean cuisine and ingredients internationally. If you ever wonder why, in the early 2010s, chefs in New York and Los Angeles "discovered" gochujang—or "Korean red pepper paste," as they called it—all at once, it's because the $90 million campaign by South Korea's Ministry of Agriculture, Food and Rural Affairs was working. Now, as hansik, or Korean cuisine, takes on myriad forms in the hands of first- and second-generation Korean American chefs around the country, jangs are being even more deeply explored and deftly used. And back home, seeing this, we take even more pride in our own jang production. The virtuous cycle continues.

Today, I'm happy to say, we're riding a wave of artisanal jang appreciation. Encouraged by the government, elementary schools in South Korea teach their students how to make jang. Young artisans are being mentored by older ones. Across the country, jangdok are filled with batches of ganjang, doenjang, and gochujang. Across the world, jangs are finding their way into the kitchens of Koreans and non-Koreans alike. Now, with every meal of fiery gochujang tteokbokki, spoonful of comforting doenjang stew, or dinner of savory ganjang bulgogi, one savors not just the most profound flavors but nearly the entire history of Korea in one bite.

HOW JANG IS MADE

Jangs are capable of great, almost endlessly variable expression. And yet there are only three physical pillars on which jangs rest: soybeans, water, and salt. Jang is so popular precisely because its ingredients are both readily available and affordable. How an artisan uses this trio of elements determines the quality, and qualities, of the jang. And with so few elements, there is nothing to hide behind. Time and space, the final two variables of jang, literally surround us. Like all fermented products, jang relies on chemical processes that unfold over hours, days, and years. Like other *naturally* fermented products, it relies on its environment for the bacteria and fungi that fuel its fermentation. It's fair to say jang artisans are less mothers to jang than midwives. This isn't meant to denigrate or minimize their contribution—the safe delivery of life is as important as its creation.

Though historically jangs were made of both meat and fish, for thousands of years, soybeans have been the primary protein. The entire process of inoculation and fermentation that makes a jang a jang has been developed to render readily available all the nutritional and sustaining properties of *Glycine max*, as the soybean is known in Latin. Today, soybeans are the second most-grown crop in Korea (barley is the first). There are 178 varieties and cultivars of soybean registered in Korea, but the majority of those used in jang production are a protein-rich yellow soybean cultivar called Taegwang (on Jeju Island, they use a rare green soybean).

Jang making begins in the fall or winter. The precursor to jang season is, naturally, the soybean harvest itself, which takes place in late October. In 2022, a total of 158,147 acres (64,000 ha) of soybeans were planted in Korea, yielding a harvest of 130,000 metric tons (for comparison, the United States produced 116,377,000 metric tons of soybeans in the same year, though much of this was used as biofuel). The year's crop is allowed to yellow in the field as the first frost hits, after which the beans are picked, shucked, sun-dried, and shipped out like durable precious yellow pearls that will keep for up to a year. Once the soybeans are delivered to the artisan, they are rinsed and then boiled. This is traditionally done in a gamasot, a large metal cauldron often nestled into a concrete or earthen platform outside with a fire underneath. It's a mash-up of a hearth and a pot, and is used for making everything from jang to dubu to stews. The process of boiling, which lasts up to six hours, not only softens the soybeans, a prerequisite for mashing them in the next step, but plays an important biochemical role as well: Raw soybeans contain a trypsin inhibitor and phytic acid, both of which prevent proper nutritional uptake in the human body; boiled soybeans do not.

GANJANG AND DOENJANG

After the soybeans are boiled, the pathways for ganjang and doenjang diverge from that of gochujang. Let's follow the journey of these first two jangs, reserving gochujang for later: Once the soybeans have been boiled, they are drained to draw out as much moisture as possible. Historically, this was done on platterlike handwoven bamboo sieves called sokuri; today, many artisans use simple plastic sieves, but the goal remains the same. Once the soybeans are workable, they are mashed in a large mortar called a jeolgu with a pestle about the size of a kayak oar called a gongi until they break down. The mash is then molded or pressed by hand into bricks about the size of a yoga block called meju.

Meju are where the magic of jang begins. They look like clay bricks and are, in fact, the building blocks of ganjang and doenjang. They will become the vehicle and vessel by which jang carries the environment around it. Once the meju are sufficiently dried, a process that depends on weather conditions but usually lasts between four and five weeks, they are introduced to rice straw, called jipuragi.

As is the case with so many elements of jang making, the jipuragi serves a dual role. First and most often, it is fashioned into a rope and functions like, well, a rope. Wrapped around each meju like ribbon on a gift or twine around a culatello, these lengths of rice straw are used to attach the meju to the rafters and pegs on which they will age. (Some artisans, however, forgo the hanging and place the meju atop a bed of jipuragi.) Regardless of how they interact, the close contact between the rice straw and the meju itself serves a more important role: to inoculate the dried soybean

block with the aspergillus fungi naturally present in the straw, which kick-starts the process of fermentation. Aspergillus is the engine of umami. In Japan, where it is called koji, aspergillus is the basis of shoyu, miso, and soju; in Korea, it is the basis of ganjang, doenjang, and gochujang, not to mention fermented beverages like makgeolli, a slightly effervescent and very delicious rice wine.

For two to six weeks, the meju sits still—or seemingly so. There is actually a whirl of activity transpiring unseen. The proteins and carbohydrates in the soybeans are being transformed and broken down by the aspergillus fungi into shorter amino acids called peptides. These peptides will eventually translate into what we call *gamchilmat*, "profound flavor," which is really the treasure of jang. Just as important, the bacteria and yeast in the ambient biome— the very air itself—are collaborating with the aspergillus to devour those carbohydrates and proteins. The unique bacterial and fungal signature is perhaps the most important factor in determining the flavor profile of a jang. And for jang artisans, it's also one of the most mercurial and mystical processes.

After another four to five weeks, depending on the weather conditions, the meju have dry-fermented enough and are ready to be transferred to onggi. Onggi are perhaps the most iconic pottery in Korea and are used for a variety of products. When onggi are used to store jang or kimchi, they are known as jangdok. Smaller jangdok are used to ferment kimchi; larger ones, which can range up to 21 gallons (80 L) in volume, are reserved for jang. The process of making onggi itself is an art form deserving protection. There are only twenty or so onggi master artisans formally recognized by Korea's Ministry of Culture, Sports and Tourism, the youngest of whom is in his fifties. Crafting onggi is a labor-intensive process that begins with kneading (and stomping on) sand-rich clay to remove air bubbles, then patiently coiling and smoothing it atop a potter's wheel to achieve the perfect form. These vessels are then dried for twenty days, coated in a glaze of leaf mold and soil, and fired in massive kilns. The entire process takes eight weeks. The size and shape of onggi vary from region to region. In the north, where it is cooler, onggi tend to be taller and narrower; in the warmer south, they tend to be wider but more squat. Importantly, onggi are fired at relatively low temperatures, around 1,500°F (800°C), which means their walls are porous, allowing air to flow in and out and the jang to breathe.

Jangdok are to jang as barrels are to whiskey or amphorae to wine, vessels of change. At the workshops of jang artisans, enormous jangdok are often lined up like soldiers in formation on an auspiciously placed well-lit terrace called a jangdokdae. Inside the jangdok, the meju finally meets its companions for the rest of its journey into jang: salt and water. The proportion and quality of each is of profound importance to the final product. Too much salt or too little water, and the jang won't ferment properly. Too little salt and too much water, and the flavor turns sour and off. Naturally, any impurities in the water will also be present in the jang, so high-quality crystalline water is necessary.

Though water and salt are the most functional elements in the jangdok, they aren't the only ones. A stick of charcoal and a few dried red chiles are frequently added just before sealing the jangdok with rice paper and closing their heavy ceramic lids. According to musok, Korea's ancient folk religion, the charcoal symbolizes purity and the red of the chile frightens away evil spirits. As is the case with folk wisdom around the world, their addition also plays an important, if historically poorly understood, role: The charcoal contains some purifying properties and the capsaicin in the chile contains some antibacterial ones. It's another happy convergence of folk custom and science.

As the jang continues to ferment, the most important ingredient becomes time. Once the meju is in the jangdok, you wait. And wait. And wait. Inside the jangdok, the meju comes alive. As the sun rises and sets and the temperature increases and decreases, the jang's transformation begins in earnest. It rises and falls within the jangdok, which is why the vessels are filled only about halfway. Mold blooms in an astonishingly diverse array of colors and textures: black, yellow, white, fuzzy, soft, hard. As the meju breaks down, opening itself to the salt and water, the bacteria and fungi are activated, assisted by the salt, the water, and the diurnal shift in temperature. Canny artisan producers know exactly where to place the jangdok to ensure ideal fluctuations in temperature and thus encourage enzyme activity.

Here again we come to a fork in the road. After roughly six to nine weeks, a choice is made, and the separation process between doenjang and ganjang ensues. A jang artisan monitors many factors within the jangdok before making this momentous decision. Some use a hydrometer to measure the salinity of the liquid as an indicator of readiness. Others open the jangdok, grab hold of the now porridgelike meju, and feel almost instinctually whether it is ready. At this juncture, the producer must choose which sort of jang to prioritize. The longer the softening meju rests in the liquid, the richer the ganjang will be, but the poorer the doenjang, as more and more amino acids are leached into the liquid. No matter the criteria, when separation comes, each jangdok is opened. The solids are removed, by hand or ladle, and placed over a large tub on sokuri. The liquid is collected and reserved. The solids are similarly collected. Both are repotted separately in jangdok. The former is on its way to becoming ganjang, the latter doenjang.

And then we wait again. Doenjang is aged for at least a few months and up to seven years. Ganjang, on the other hand, can be aged from just a few months up to nearly a decade. Legally, commercial ganjang must be aged for one year; doenjang has no legal minimum. By custom, most artisanal jangs sold in Korea have been aged somewhere between three and ten years.

The longer the bacteria and fungi are allowed to work, the more they break down longer polypeptides into shorter amino acids, and the deeper the jang's flavor becomes. At a certain point, when the yeast is exhausted, the fermentation is complete. But even then, bacterial activity still flourishes, causing the aromas to shift like light behind a stained-glass window. A ganjang at one year will be robustly salty; at three, it is sweeter, and at five, sweeter still. A doenjang follows the same trajectory, trading in saltiness for increased gamchilmat.

GOCHUJANG

Chances are, if you've heard about jang at all, you know about gochujang, which is funny, since gochujang is an outlier in some ways. It also makes sense that when the Korean government chose to promote "the next kimchi," gochujang was first in line for international recognition. Fermented soybeans are used throughout Asia, and though there are substantial differences, ganjang is not too dissimilar from shoyu or doenjang from miso; gochujang, however, is uniquely, irrevocably, intimately Korean. That's because its signature ingredient, the gochu chile, grows here exclusively. Green when unripe and growing redder with time, these small peppers are mild, only about 1,000 to 1,500 Scoville units (by comparison, jalapeños come in at 2,000 Scoville units and habaneros range from 150,000 to 575,000), with a touch of sweetness. Though some theories posit that the gochu chile arrived in Korea in the sixteenth century, brought by Portuguese traders through Japan, recently scientists have surmised that it was actually introduced by birds millions of years ago. (Birds, interestingly, do not have the taste receptor to sense spiciness and are therefore key eaters and distributors of pepper seeds.)

Like all jang, gochujang relies on soybeans as its base. However, whereas the other jangs are triads consisting of soybeans, salt, and water, gochujang has many more notes. Part of what is so intoxicating about gochujang is the sheer number of variables. The additions include rice, glutinous rice powder, rice syrup, barley malt, and, of course, gochu powder.

Gochujang meju differ from other jang meju in both shape and composition. Whereas for ganjang and doenjang only soybeans are formed into the meju, for gochujang, rice and soybeans are boiled separately and mixed in a 4:6 ratio, then pressed into meju. Gochujang meju tend to be formed into smaller blocks, or sometimes

balls about the size of a baseball. Once dried, these are strung up with jipuragi and left to ferment on their own for three weeks. (With their carb-rich rice, gochujang meju mold more quickly than the meju used for making ganjang and doenjang.) In this way, gochujang also captures the microflora of the environment and is just as capable of expressing terroir as ganjang and doenjang are.

Instead of being flung directly into the jangdok, the meju are pulverized into a powder called meju garu (*garu* simply means "powder" or "meal"). This powder is added to a mixture of glutinous rice powder and some sort of sweetener—often milled malted barley or rice syrup—that has been heated to break down the carbohydrates into sugars, a process called saccharification. Finally, the gochugaru is added and only then is the mixture placed in the jangdok. Like all jang, at this point it must be left alone, to increase and decrease, to expand in the heat and contract in the cold. All the while enzymes are working their magic.

Gochujang artisans vary the proportions of each element, including how high and for how long the mixture is heated and for how long the mixture sits to cool (and ferment) at each step. Some artisans use ganjang instead of salt. Others use steamed glutinous rice itself, not just its powdered form. Grains can vary from brown rice to barley and sorghum. Many artisans use seasonal local ingredients like strawberry gochujang from Chungnam Province in the southwest. Perhaps the most recognizable change is the degree of heat, a function of how much gochugaru is added. The most important thing is to foster the full flowering of both the aspergillus and the bacteria, allowing them to do their fermentation work.

Gochujang can be ready to eat after six months, but most is sold after aging for one year. More time in the jangdok naturally mellows out the spiciness, lowers the acidity, and deepens the flavor. However, unlike in doenjang and ganjang production, extending the length of time to years doesn't necessarily pay dividends. After just one year, the fermentation is complete, and the gochujang emerges spicy, sweet, salty, and utterly addictive.

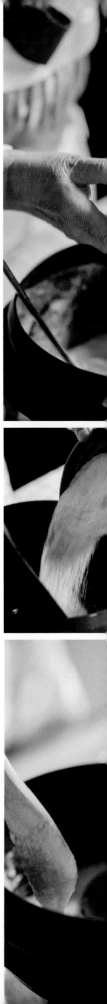

HOW TO USE THIS BOOK

This book is divided into three sections—Ganjang, Doenjang, and Gochujang—with recipes organized based on which type of jang they showcase the most. But as you'll see, the jangs are like siblings, and like siblings, they often play together. Don't feel as if you need to cook from only one section at a time. Flip through the pages, find something you think looks delicious, and make it. Even better, find a couple of things that look delicious and make them.

Within each section, recipes are arranged from lightest to most substantial, progressing from vegetables and salads to soups and stews to rice and noodle dishes; seafood, meat, and poultry; and finally desserts. This will not come as a particular surprise to anyone who has used a cookbook before. However, this is also a cookbook based on how Koreans eat, both at home and out, so it might be useful to know something about that before you begin your adventures in jang.

There are generally two ways of sequencing a meal: one is through time, and the other is through space. The Western meal progression is a linear one through time. There are appetizers, salads, soups, a pasta, perhaps, and then a main course. The dishes are doled out one by one as the meal unfurls. The finer the meal, the longer the chain of dishes served.

Korean meals take place not on a temporal plane but on a spatial one. Everything everywhere all at once. Think of the Western style of eating a meal as like a parade. Bansang, as the traditional Korean way of enjoying a meal is known, is more like a circle of friends conversing. Naturally, this affects how we cook, too. Since each dish is meant to be enjoyed with others, there is, to me, a beautiful interdependence among them. No one dish carries the meal on its own.

It is hardly surprising that bansang was developed during the Joseon dynasty, the heavily Confucian-influenced, order-obsessed long-running regime that ruled Korea from the fourteenth century

to the twentieth. Traditionally, bansang was, like everything else at that time, dictated by social rank. At the very minimum, bansang consisted of bap (rice), guk (soup) or jjigae (stew), jang, kimchi, and three banchan, or side dishes. This was called 3 cheop bansang. The core elements never shifted—there was always a bap, a guk or jjigae, a jang, and a kimchi—but the number of banchan increased with social rank from three to five to seven to nine and, finally, for royalty, to twelve. The delicately made side dishes spanned the flavor continuum from spicy to salty to sweet to fermented. They were like a palette of colors with which each diner could paint their own picture.

In this book, you won't find royal court cuisine with an expansive retinue of banchan. The recipes are instead a combination of traditional Korean dishes I grew up with and love to make for my family and friends and more Western-influenced recipes that really showcase how jang belongs in the world pantry. Even in the most traditional houses, not every Korean meal is served in the bansang style today. Many, just like Western meals, are one-pot or one-plate affairs. This is especially true of dishes like bibimbap, where the rice is already incorporated into the recipe.

That said, many of the recipes you'll find in these pages have traditionally been served as part of bansang. And you can use these recipes to prepare an excellent 3 cheop bansang spread, so I think it's useful to know how you can combine them to create your own bansang. (See page 42 for a guide.) What I suggest is picking two or three banchan, one guk or jjigae, and one main course (from either the traditional or versatile list sections below) to prepare. Alternatively, pick one or two banchan plus a versatile or Western-style main course. Just like hangul, the Korean alphabet, bansang is modular and easy to use. Traditionally, when serving banchan you would never repeat cooking styles. So if you were going to feature steamed vegetables in one banchan, you would not repeat that technique in the others you planned to serve. But can we all agree that's a bit excessive? These days, the most important guideline is to not double up flavors.

MIX AND MATCH THESE DISHES TO MAKE A MEAL

BANCHAN

Jangajji (Preserved Vegetables in Jang) 59

Broccolini Namul 63

Green Beans with Sesame Vinaigrette 112

Cucumber Muchim 160

Ganjang Saewoo Jang
(Ganjang-Marinated Shrimp) 88

Root Vegetable Salad 115

GUK AND JJIGAE

Miyeok Guk (Seaweed Soup) 71

Baechu Sogogi Doenjang Jeongol
(Cabbage Beef Doenjang Stew) 121

Honghap Doenjang Guk
(Mussel Doenjang Soup) 127

Gochujang Jjigae
(Gochujang Stew) 167

MAIN COURSES

Haemul Pajeon
(Seafood Scallion Pancake) 87

Galbijjim (Braised Short Ribs) 92

Japchae (Glass Noodles with
Mixed Vegetables) 78

Godeung-eo Jorim
(Ganjang-Braised Mackerel) 91

LA Galbi Gui (LA-Style Grilled
Short Ribs) 95

Tteokgalbi (Short Rib Burgers) 96

Samgyeopsal Suyuk-gwa Musaengchae
(Boiled Pork Belly with Quick Daikon
Kimchi) 139

Dakbokkeumtang
(Spicy Chicken Stew) 169

Mandu Jeongol
(Korean Dumpling Hotpot) 73

Jae-Yuk Bokkeum
(Gochujang-Marinated Stir-Fried Pork) 192

VERSATILE MAIN COURSES

Gochujang Hwe Muchim
(Snapper Crudo with Chogochujang
Dressing) 185

Yangnyeom Chicken
(Korean Fried Chicken) 171

Doenjang BBQ Lamb with Couscous 141

Gochujang BBQ Cookout 189

WESTERN MAIN COURSES

Steamed Cod with Doenjang Béarnaise 132

Dover Sole with Doenjang Caper Sauce 135

Ssamjang Cacio e Pepe 130

THE KOREAN PANTRY

Korean cooking, perhaps more than most of the world's cuisines, is heavily dependent on the pantry. We Koreans have always been pragmatic, practical people, looking for ways to save time cooking while still achieving a profound depth of flavor. Many of these pantry items are the secrets to gamchilmat—profound flavor—in a dish. Like umami, gamchilmat is often the product of fermentation, which is itself a method of leveraging time for flavor. Other pantry items are simply kitchen staples that you'll find useful (and necessary) not just in these recipes but hopefully when you're cooking on the fly, too.

JANGS

The most important items in your pantry, for our purposes, are going to be your jangs. Here's what's on the market, what to look for, and what to buy when it comes to ganjang, doenjang, and gochujang. (For a complete list of recommendations, see Resources, page 205.)

Ganjang

For the most part, this book is concerned with artisanal jang, the most interesting and flavorful variety. But not everything can be artisanal, nor is it always worth using (or even a good idea to use) artisanal jang in every dish you make. In Korea, we have three types of ganjang: yangjo, hansik, and jin. Off

the bat, avoid jin ganjang. *Jin* means "deep, dark color," which, in jin ganjang, is achieved through an industrialized chemical process first used by the Japanese during their occupation of Korea in the late nineteenth century to make cheap soy sauce for their troops. Jin ganjang is not fermented but instead is made by boiling soybeans in hydrochloric acid, filtering and purifying the liquefied beans, then adding coloring agents, flavoring agents, and preservatives. It looks like ganjang and tastes vaguely like it, but it is not truly ganjang.

As for whether to choose yangjo or hansik ganjang, it isn't really a question of "either/or" but of "both/and," since both varieties are essential ingredients.

Yangjo Ganjang

Yangjo ganjang, or "brewed ganjang," is by far the most widely used type of ganjang in Korea. It can be made relatively cheaply on a large scale. Whereas artisanal ganjang is made with naturally fermented blocks of meju, yangjo ganjang is made with a slurry of defatted soybeans, a by-product of the soybean oil production process, in combination with fungi—*Aspergillus oryzae* or *Aspergillus sojae*—and carefully introduced bacteria. Sempio, for instance, one of the largest jang makers, has three fridges in its headquarters filled with bacteria. Because all variables are controlled, yangjo ganjang is much easier to make, quite standardized, and more affordable.

Tastewise, yangjo ganjang tends to be crisper and cleaner than artisanal ganjang.

I choose yangjo ganjang primarily when I'm using it in a braise, brine, or marinade. That is, when I need a lot of it but the ganjang itself is not being directly consumed. Some of the most common and highest-quality yangjo ganjangs are Sempio's 501 and 701 series. The numbers represent the total nitrogen (TN) value of the ganjang, which relates directly to its soybean content. The higher the value, the better the ganjang: 501 has a TN of 1.5 percent; 701 a value of 1.7 percent. I have liters of both at home, stored in a cool, dry place.

Hansik Ganjang

Hansik ganjang is the best and highest expression of ganjang. Also called Joseon ganjang, guk ganjang, or jaerae ganjang, hansik ganjang is made by artisans according to traditional methods. (For more on these methods, see page 30.) More expensive, with a broad variation in flavor, hansik ganjang is like the extra-virgin olive oil of jang; I use it when the jang itself is being showcased, as is the case with guk (soup) and namul (vegetables), as well as in vinaigrettes and delicate sauces. It is noticeably saltier and more savory than yangjo ganjang.

With such a spectrum of flavors, choosing a hansik ganjang really becomes a matter of personal preference. Some, like the product made by Amisan Sookti, are nearly meaty; others, like Mcgguroom, are clean, with a bristling salinity. The flavors depend on many factors, including how the jang is made, how it is stored, and how long it is aged. One of my favorite parts of the jang journey is to taste as widely as I can; I hope you do the same.

Whereas just a few years ago, it would have been impossible to get hansik ganjang in the United States, today there are many options available. Among my favorite brands are Mcgguroom Golden Joseon Ganjang, made by a wonderful artisan in the park-filled area of Cheongsong, in the eastern part of Korea (see page 151); Baekmalsoon, from Seongju, in the south; and Kisoondo, which is made by a tenth-generation jang master in the bamboo forests of Damyang.

Doenjang

Doenjang comes in both yangjo and hansik varieties as well (there is no such thing as jin doenjang, thankfully). The breakdown for usage is similar to that of ganjang. When doenjang itself is the star, as in soups and stews, use hansik or artisanal doenjang. When the doenjang is used as a flavor influence, as in a braise or marinade, yangjo doenjang is fine. When you want a mixture of mild and intensely flavored doenjang, you can always mix the two (see Building a Jang Pantry, page 52).

Yangjo Doenjang

Yangjo doenjang is generally called original doenjang or simply doenjang. Like yangjo ganjang, it is made from defatted soybeans to which yeast and bacterial cultures are introduced. As always, the best guideline is to look for the shortest ingredient list. Try to avoid added wheat, sugars, preservatives, or artificial colors.

The best and most readily available brand is CJ Haechandle, which uses a blend of bacterial agents and cultured yeasts. Another great option is Chung Jung One's Sunchang doenjang, alternately labeled as "Sunchang soybean paste."

Hansik Doenjang

Generally speaking, jang artisans make both ganjang and doenjang, since one is the by-product of the other. Therefore, most producers of hansik ganjang also sell a line of hansik doenjang. Hansik doenjangs range from more intensely savory to less so. One of my favorite producers, Mcgguroom (see page 151), makes both a wonderful hansik ganjang and a delicious hansik doenjang called Golden Mac Doenjang.

Gochujang

As the most popular jang abroad, gochujang presents many options. Most brands are made in Korea, but there is a rising number of artisans making gochujang in the United States as well. Unlike doenjang and ganjang, gochujang traditionally isn't classified as yangjo or hansik, which makes determining which one to buy a little more difficult.

In terms of quality, just as with other jangs, a short list of ingredients is a good indicator. Gochujang contains more ingredients than its cousins, ganjang and doenjang. These can include glutinous rice powder, wheat flour, soybean powder

producers has standardized their hotness scale with something called the Gochujang Hot-Taste Unit (GHU). Based on the amount of capsaicin, an active chemical component in chile peppers, the heat scale contains five levels: mildly hot (1), slightly hot (2), medium hot (3), very hot (4), and extremely hot (5). Since gochu peppers are themselves relatively mild, with a Scoville level of no more than 1,500, any gochujang equal to or above very hot (GHU 4) generally includes the spicier Cheongyang chile pepper to boost the spice level.

I prefer gochujang on the mildly to slightly hot (GHU 1 or 2) side. I want a gochujang that still allows me to enjoy a glass of wine with my meal. (Wine might be the only thing I love as much as jang.) Anything that burns my palate through is too spicy and will overpower all that will come after it.

Two of my favorite widely available gochujang brands are CJ Haechandle and Chung Jung One, which is made with brown rice syrup. However, to really get a sense of gochujang's promise, seek out artisanal gochujang. The best gochujang in Korea comes from Sunchang, a region in the southwest famous for its gochujang (for more on Sunchang, see page 199). Among the best gochujangs on the market are those from seventh-generation certified master artisans Sunchang Moon Ok-Rye and Kang Soon-Ok, whose jangs are well balanced with sweetness, saltiness, and spice.

(also called meju powder), and gochugaru (sometimes listed as "red pepper powder," "Korean red pepper powder," or "Korean pepper powder"). Most gochujang has some sort of sweetener added, too, either sugar, malt syrup, grain syrup, or corn syrup. If you want a more savory, and also better, jang, look for brands whose ingredient lists do not include corn syrup as the second or third ingredient.

The quality of chile used is of paramount importance when choosing a gochujang. Look for brands that use sun-dried red chiles, which will be listed as "taeyangcho." Try to avoid gochujang that uses "red pepper seasoning," which is *not* gochugaru at all but rather a mixture of onion, garlic, and Chinese chile.

The level of heat is a personal preference. Since 2010, a consortium of major jang

OTHER STAPLES

Jangs are necessary and foundational components of building a Korean pantry but not the only ingredients you'll need or make frequent use of throughout this book. The following staples—from important ones like rice to lesser-known components like perilla oil—complete your home pantry.

Aekjeot

Aekjeot is a Korean fish sauce. Made with salted and dried fish, aekjeot itself is derived from jeotgal, a long-hallowed class of salted seafood, of which there are more than fifty varieties. In fact, *aekjeot* means simply "liquid jeotgal." Today there are two main types of aekjeot: myeolchi aekjeot, made with anchovies; and the milder kkanari aekjeot, made with sand lance fish, a small, rather cute creature that buries itself in the sand and feeds on tiny microorganisms. Whereas jang is filled with vegetable-derived MSG, aekjeot is rich with natural MSG derived from animal protein. On its own, aekjeot adds gamchilmat without any fermented flavors. In combination with jang, it adds another layer of flavor to the foundations of soups, salads, and stocks.

Brown Rice Vinegar

What balsamic vinegar is to Italy and white wine vinegar is to France, brown rice vinegar is to Korea. Much more widely used than simple rice vinegar, brown rice vinegar imparts a sweet-and-sour flavor to many dishes, from salads to dressings for seafood. (We do have a white rice vinegar, usually made from the rice wine makgeolli, but it is higher in acidity and has a more heavily fermented scent.)

Frying Batter Mix

The secret to Korean fried chicken (see page 171) is jang. But the secret to the coating is this batter mix, made with a combination of flour, cornstarch, baking powder, and a bunch of spices (onion powder, black pepper, garlic powder). My favorite brand is CJ Beksul shrimp tempura frying mix. It contains a healthy dose of spices and no added sugar, and yields the perfect crispy texture and a golden coat. If you can't find it, don't worry—it's easy to make a homemade version to keep on hand.

Homemade Frying Batter Mix

Makes approximately 7 cups (915 g)

7 cups (880 g) all-purpose flour
1 tablespoon plus 1 teaspoon garlic powder
1 tablespoon plus 1 teaspoon onion powder
1 teaspoon kosher salt

Into an airtight container, sift together the flour, garlic powder, onion powder, and salt. Store in a cool, dry place for up to 3 months.

Perilla Oil

Like sesame oil, perilla oil is made from toasted seeds, this time of the perilla plant, whose beautiful serrated leaves make their way into soups, lettuce wraps known as ssam, and stir-fries. When milled into an oil, the seeds have an earthier flavor and a gentler, more rounded aroma than sesame seeds. Popular in the southern end of the peninsula, where the plant grows in abundance, perilla oil is often used interchangeably with sesame oil, though I prefer perilla oil for more delicate dishes where the oil is not cooked, like Kimchi Bibim Guksu (Kimchi Mixed Noodles with Gochujang Sauce; page 179) and Yukhwe Bibimbap (Beef Tartare Bibimbap; page 176).

Powders (Garu)

Because Korean cooking is so heavily reliant on soups, stews, sauces, and pastes, powders—which allow a spice or ingredient to quickly and seamlessly dissolve into a liquid—are key ingredients in the pantry.

Gochugaru

Gochugaru is by far the most important powder in the Korean pantry. It is the key ingredient in gochujang as well as in kimchi, but its uses don't stop there. Gochugaru naturally adds heat to many soups and stews, from spicy chicken stew to beef doenjang soup. There are two types of gochugaru you should have: finely ground and coarsely ground. I use the finely ground powder for thicker sauces and pastes and on cold dishes like steamed and seasoned vegetables (namul). I use the coarsely ground gochugaru in broths (the finely ground powder tends to make broths cloudy).

Doenjang Powder

Doenjang powder is not a very common ingredient in most Korean cooking, but it is in mine. I use doenjang in its powdered form like a seasoning salt. It adds gamchilmat and saltiness, with less sodium than your regular table salt.

To make 1.75 ounces (50 g) doenjang powder, spread 3.5 ounces (100 g) doenjang in a very thin layer on a parchment paper–lined baking sheet and dry in a convection oven at 160°F (70°C) for 6 hours. Grind the dried doenjang into a fine powder using a mortar and pestle. Store in an airtight container in the freezer for up to 3 months or at room temperature for up to 1 month.

Gochujang Powder

Like doenjang powder, gochujang powder is not a common store-bought ingredient but is one that I find essential. Whereas gochugaru adds heat and doenjang powder adds saltiness and gamchilmat, gochujang powder adds all three. I sprinkle it on everything from french fries and popcorn to biscuit sandwiches.

To make 2.5 ounces (70 g) gochujang powder, spread 3.5 ounces (100 g) gochujang in a very thin layer on a parchment paper–lined baking sheet and dry in a convection oven at 160°F (70°C) for 6 hours, then flip the almost-dried gochujang and dry for 6 hours more. Grind the dried gochujang into a fine powder using a mortar and pestle. Store in an airtight container in the freezer for up to 3 months or at room temperature for up to 1 month.

Rice

You're going to want to eat rice with your meal. Rice is so important to Koreans that one way of saying "How are you doing?" is to ask "Have you eaten your rice?" A meal without rice is not a meal. So it is almost unspoken—but not unwritten—that for all the bansang here, you'll need to make rice. The only exceptions are dishes that already contain rice, such as Gangdoenjang Bibimbap (page 129), or ones that include other carbs, like Ssamjang Cacio e Pepe (page 130). I recommend ½ to ¾ cup (100 to 150 g) cooked rice per person. Ideally, you'll have a rice cooker—most kitchens in Korea have one—but I've included a recipe for making rice in a cast-iron pot in the event that you don't.

Rice (in a Rice Cooker)

Makes 4¾ cups (950 g), 4 to 5 servings

2½ cups (500 g) uncooked medium-grain white rice

Rinse the rice in a large bowl with cold water. Drain and repeat, gently rubbing the rice in the water. Repeat this process two or three times, until the water in the bowl is clear.

Drain the rice in a sieve, then weigh it. Subtract 17.5 ounces (500 grams, the original weight of the dry rice), in order to see how much water has been absorbed by the rice already. Subtract the resulting amount from 19.5 ounces (550 g) water.

Place the rice in the rice cooker, then add the water. Smooth the rice out, then cook the rice according to the manufacturer's instructions.

Note: If you're making less than 2½ cups (500 g) rice, increase the cooking water by 1 tablespoon.

Rice (on the Stovetop)

Makes 4¾ cups (950 g), 4 to 5 servings

2½ cups (500 g) uncooked medium-grain white rice

Rinse the rice in a large bowl with cold water. Drain and repeat, gently rubbing the rice in the water. Repeat this process two or three times, until the water in the bowl is clear.

Drain the rice in a sieve, then weigh it. Subtract 17.5 ounces (500 grams, the original weight of the dry rice), in order to see how much water has been absorbed by the rice already. Subtract the resulting amount from 21 ounces (600 g) water.

Place the rice in a large cast-iron pot with a lid and add the water. Cover and bring the water to a boil over medium heat, about 5 minutes, then open the lid and scrape the bottom of the pot once or twice so the rice doesn't stick. Cover, reduce the heat to low, and cook for 15 minutes. Remove from the heat and let sit, covered, for 10 minutes more.

When the rice is done, use a rice spatula to stir the finished rice up and down evenly.

Sesame Oil

Like fermented foods, sesame oil binds all Korean cooking together. In Korea, as in Japan and China, we use toasted sesame oil. Much of the distinctly roasted and nutty flavors emerge as a result of how the sesame seeds are roasted, as well as regional variations in the sesame itself. In Korea, sesame oil is used mostly as a finishing oil. It has a powerful flavor, however, and should be utilized with care. When purchasing sesame oil, make sure to look for brands that use 100% whole sesame seeds, not simply sesame seed powder.

Toasted Sesame Seeds

Since nuts grow only seldom in Korea, we rely on toasted seeds to give our food its nutty flavor. Toasted sesame seeds are omnipresent in Korean kitchens, and we use them both as a garnish and to add flavor in everything from namul to bokkeum to salads. Whole sesame seeds can be used as a garnish, but when cooking, it is best to use ground sesame seeds. Buy your sesame seeds whole and grind them to order using a mortar and pestle or a sesame seed grinder; otherwise, you'll lose out on their delicate nutty flavor.

Stocks

A whole book could, and probably should, be written on the role of stocks in Korean cooking. They, like jangs, are integral in the underpainting of flavor that renders Korean cuisine so remarkably rich. But this is not that book, so I've narrowed the field to two basic stocks: chicken and anchovy.

Though the chicken stock is rather standard, similar to one you might find in the kitchen of any French chef, anchovy stock is rather more unique to the East. Using kelp to add gamchilmat, this flavorful broth is often used in tandem with heavier stocks like beef stock, as in Baechu Sogogi Doenjang Jeongol (Cabbage Beef Doenjang Stew, page 121), to lighten the overall dish without sacrificing any flavor.

Chicken Stock

Makes 4½ cups (1.1 L)

1 (3- to 4-pound/1 kg) whole chicken
About 10 green onions, cut into ½-inch (1 cm) pieces
5 whole black peppercorns
3 garlic cloves, peeled

Rinse the chicken well under cold water. Remove any internal organs and any trace of blood. Trim any excess fat attached to the tail.

Place the chicken, green onions, peppercorns, and garlic in a large soup pot, then pour in 4½ cups (1.1 L) cold water. Bring to a boil over medium heat, skimming any impurities from the top. Reduce the heat to maintain a simmer and cook, skimming the top occasionally, for 1½ hours.

Line a sieve with cheesecloth and place it over a large container. Strain the stock through the prepared sieve and discard the chicken, as all the flavor will be extracted, or pick the meat and use it for other dishes. Either place the container in an ice bath to cool it quickly or simply allow the broth to cool to room temperature. Cover and refrigerate for 3 to 4 hours, until completely cool, then remove the layer of hardened fat from the surface. The stock will keep in the fridge for up to 3 days or in an airtight container in the freezer for up to 3 months.

Anchovy Stock

Makes 5 cups (1.2 L)

3.5 ounces (100 g) large dried whole anchovies
6 green onions, cut into ½-inch (1 cm) pieces
⅓ peeled daikon radish, cut into ½-inch (1 cm) cubes
1 (6-inch/15 cm) square piece dried kelp (10 g)

Remove the guts from the anchovies and discard. Warm a pan over high heat and add the anchovies. Cook, stirring continuously, for 5 minutes to remove any residual moisture. (Do not let the anchovies burn.) Remove the anchovies and let them cool. (Alternatively, place the anchovies in a small bowl and microwave for about a minute, stirring them every 15 to 30 seconds to make sure they don't burn. Remove and let cool.)

Place the anchovies, green onions, daikon, and kelp in a large soup pot and add 8⅓ cups (2 L) cold water. Bring the water to a boil over medium heat, skimming any impurities from the top. Reduce the heat to maintain a simmer and cook, skimming occasionally, for 30 minutes, until the vegetables are soft.

Line a sieve with cheesecloth and place it over a large container. Strain the stock through the prepared sieve. Either place the container in an ice bath to cool it quickly or simply allow the broth to cool to room temperature. The stock will keep in the fridge for up to 3 days or in an airtight container in the freezer for up to 3 months.

OTHER EQUIPMENT

Steamer

You can make your own stovetop steamer by perching a plate on three balls of tinfoil within a larger pot, adding 1 inch (2.5 cm) of water to the pot, covering it, and then heating—but it will be worth your while to purchase a good two- or three-tier stainless steel steamer with a glass lid. There's a lot of steaming in this book, and you'll soon make up the cost in terms of both time and tinfoil if you invest in a proper steamer.

BUILDING A JANG PANTRY

Think of jangs as primary colors. They are strong on their own but often benefit from mixing. Jangs are frequently combined with either each other or additional ingredients to form a stable of frequently used variants. Some, like ssamjang, are well-known; others are less so. Some, like vinegary chogochujang, can be bought at the supermarket, although, as you'll see here, they're so easy to make at home—why not try?

All these sauces keep well in the refrigerator. (If you cook from this book, you'll run out of them before they go bad.) I recommend spending no more than an hour or so creating your arsenal of jang, then keeping these sauces at hand as you move through the book. Not every recipe uses one of these variations, but many do. Traditionally, these mixtures are made using ratios based on weight (in grams). This allows you to scale them up or down.

NOTE: We've used weight ratios, but if you'd prefer to measure by volume, we've included those equivalents as well. Just be aware that the ratios will not apply to volume measurements.

Light Mat-Ganjang

Mat-ganjang is a sweetened seasoned ganjang best used for vegetables, seafood, and lighter proteins.

Makes 1.2 kilograms

RATIO: 4 parts yangjo ganjang, 1 part sugar, 1 part water

800 grams yangjo ganjang
200 grams sugar
200 grams water

Combine the ganjang, sugar, and water in a pot. Bring to a boil over medium heat, then remove from the heat and let cool. Store in an airtight container in the refrigerator for up to 1 month.

TO MEASURE BY VOLUME
3 cups yangjo ganjang
1 cup sugar
1/2 cup plus 1/3 cup water

Dark Mat-Ganjang

Similar to light mat-ganjang, this variation uses brown sugar for a stronger flavor. It is best used for techniques in which the sugar can caramelize, like grilling, or for braising.

Makes 1.3 kilograms

RATIO: 6 parts yangjo ganjang, 4 parts water, 3 parts brown sugar

600 grams yangjo ganjang
400 grams water
300 grams brown sugar

Combine the ganjang, water, and brown sugar in a pot. Bring to a boil over medium heat, then remove from the heat and let cool. Store in an airtight container in the refrigerator for 2 to 3 months.

TO MEASURE BY VOLUME
2 1/4 cups yangjo ganjang
1 2/3 cups water
1 1/2 cups packed brown sugar

Blended Doenjang

This version of doenjang combines both yangjo and hansik doenjangs for a milder flavor. It's best and often used with seasoned steamed vegetables (namul) or in soups (guk) and stews (jjigae).

Makes 280 grams

RATIO: 1 part yangjo doenjang, 1 part hansik doenjang

140 grams yangjo doenjang
140 grams hansik doenjang

Mix both doenjangs together well in a small bowl. Pass through a sieve to make sure there are no larger bean parts in the mixture. Store in an airtight container in the refrigerator for up to 3 months.

TO MEASURE BY VOLUME
1/2 cup yangjo doenjang
1/2 cup hansik doenjang

Ssamjang

Ssamjang, one of hansik's most commonly used dipping sauces, is a slightly sweet, slightly spicy, and deeply flavorful condiment most famously used for boiled pork belly (see page 139), where the combination of acid and spice cuts through the pork's fattiness.

Makes 160 grams

RATIO: 10 parts yangjo doenjang, 5 parts gochujang, 1 part sugar

100 grams yangjo doenjang
50 grams gochujang
10 grams sugar

Combine the doenjang, gochujang, and sugar in a bowl and mix well until the sugar has dissolved. Store in an airtight container in the refrigerator for up to 3 months.

TO MEASURE BY VOLUME
1/3 cup yangjo doenjang
3 tablespoons gochujang
1 teaspoon sugar

BBQ Doenjang

Doenjang is often used as a dipping sauce or as an element to be dissolved into a liquid, such as a soup. But sometimes it can be used as a glaze itself. In that case, this sauce, which both sweetens the doenjang and thins it, is perfect.

Makes 640 grams

RATIO: 6 parts yangjo doenjang, 2 parts water, 1 part sugar, 1 part oil

600 grams yangjo doenjang
200 grams water
100 grams sugar
100 grams neutral oil, such as grapeseed
   or canola

Combine the doenjang, water, and sugar in a pot. Bring to a boil over medium heat, then reduce the heat to maintain a simmer and cook, stirring continuously, for 15 to 20 minutes, until the volume has reduced by about 60 percent. Add the oil and mix well. Let cool, then store in an airtight container in the refrigerator for up to 3 months.

TO MEASURE BY VOLUME
2 cups plus 2 tablespoons yangjo doenjang
1/2 cup plus 1/3 cup water
1/2 cup sugar
1/2 cup neutral oil, such as grapeseed or
   canola

Chogochujang

With its combination of spiciness, sweetness, and acidity, chogochujang—*cho* means "vinegar"—is the perfect complement for seafood and sashimi.

Makes 550 grams

RATIO: 8 parts gochujang, 2 parts vinegar, 1 part sugar

400 grams gochujang
100 grams rice vinegar
50 grams sugar

Combine the gochujang, vinegar, and sugar in a bowl and mix well until the sugar has dissolved. Store in an airtight container in the refrigerator for up to 1 month.

TO MEASURE BY VOLUME
1 1/3 cups gochujang
1/3 cup plus 1 tablespoon rice vinegar
1/4 cup sugar

Sauté Gochujang

This sauce helps thin out gochujang when sautéing or stir-frying, while the addition of sugar facilitates caramelization.

Makes 600 grams

RATIO: 4 parts gochujang, 1 part yangjo ganjang, 1 part sugar

400 grams gochujang
100 grams yangjo ganjang
100 grams sugar

Combine the gochujang, ganjang, and sugar in a bowl and mix well until the sugar has dissolved. Store in an airtight container in the refrigerator for up to 3 months.

TO MEASURE BY VOLUME
1 1/3 cups gochujang
1/3 cup plus 1 tablespoon yangjo ganjang
1/2 cup sugar

BBQ Gochujang

Combining gochujang with ganjang, sugar, and oil, this sauce turns it into a perfect marinade for meats, which works especially well for pork.

Makes 1.5 kilograms

RATIO: 6 parts gochujang, 4 parts yangjo ganjang, 4 parts sugar, 1 part oil

600 grams gochujang
400 grams yangjo ganjang
400 grams sugar
100 grams neutral oil, such as grapeseed or
   canola

Combine the gochujang, ganjang, sugar, and oil in a pot over medium heat. Stirring continuously, bring to a boil. Remove from the heat and let cool. Store in the refrigerator for up to 3 months.

TO MEASURE BY VOLUME
2 cups gochujang
1½ cups yangjo ganjang
2 cups sugar
½ cup neutral oil, such as grapeseed or
   canola

GANJANG

JANGAJJI 장아찌
Preserved Vegetables in Jang

Pickling as preservation is a near universal strategy, a way to keep the spring and summer bounties long after the warmth and harvest fades. Traditionally, vegetables would be preserved in ganjang, doenjang, and gochujang—the "jang" in *jangajji*—over a long period of time, so the result was both fermented *and* pickled. This modern jangajji, however, relies on vinegar (cho) to speed up the process. The result doesn't have the fermented tang of, say, kimchi but still bears a bracing tart streak. Though often included in banchan, jangajji is more of a condiment than a freestanding element. Its tartness cuts through rich proteins. Pair it with pork barbecue or place some atop a cheeseburger.

NOTE: As in Building a Jang Pantry (see page 52), it's more important to understand the ratio or relationship between ganjang, vinegar, sugar, and water than it is to follow a spelled-out recipe, so this brine is often made based on a ratio by weight. We've followed that convention here, but have also included volume measurements for convenience. Just keep in mind that the ratios do not hold when measuring by volume.

Brine for Leafy or Soft Vegetables

MAKES 1.5 KILOGRAMS

RATIO: 6 parts water,
4 parts yangjo ganjang,
1 part sugar, 4 parts vinegar

600 grams water
400 grams yangjo ganjang
100 grams sugar
400 grams rice vinegar

TO MEASURE BY VOLUME

2½ cups water
1⅔ cups rice vinegar
1½ cups yangjo ganjang
½ cup sugar

Combine the water, ganjang, and sugar in a small pot. Bring to a boil, then remove from the heat and let cool. Add the vinegar. While the brine is cooling, clean the vegetables well. (Cut them into chunks, if desired.) When the brine is completely cool, pour it into a sterilized airtight container. Press the vegetables into the brine until all are submerged. Cover and refrigerate.

Herbs and cherry tomatoes will be ready to use in 1 day.

Rhubarb, celery, cucumber, white asparagus, Broccolini, and bell peppers will be ready in 2 to 3 days.

Ramps, pearl onions, shallots, green tomatoes, cauliflower, and wild chives will be ready in 5 days.

The pickled vegetables will keep in the refrigerator for up to 1 year.

Brine for Firm Vegetables

MAKES 800 GRAMS

RATIO: 3 parts water, 2 parts yangjo ganjang, 1 part sugar, 2 parts vinegar

300 grams water
200 grams yangjo ganjang
100 grams sugar
200 grams rice vinegar

Combine the water, ganjang, and sugar in a small pot. Bring to a boil, then remove from the heat and let cool. Add the vinegar. While the brine is cooling, clean the vegetables well. (Cut them into chunks, if desired.) When the brine is completely cool, pour it into a sterilized airtight container. Press the vegetables into the brine until all are submerged. Cover and refrigerate.

Diced sunchokes, radishes, onions, mushrooms, garlic, and burdock will be ready in 3 to 5 days. Whole vegetables will be ready in 3 to 4 weeks.

The pickled vegetables will keep in the refrigerator for up to 1 year.

TO MEASURE BY VOLUME

1¼ cups water
¾ cup plus 1 tablespoon rice vinegar
¾ cup yangjo ganjang
½ cup sugar

BROCCOLINI NAMUL

브로콜리니 나물

SERVES 2

9 ounces (250 g)
Broccolini or Japanese
angelica shoots

1 tablespoon plus
2 teaspoons kosher salt

1 tablespoon plus
2 teaspoons hansik
ganjang

4 teaspoons toasted
sesame oil

1 teaspoon sesame seeds,
ground, plus a pinch of
whole seeds for garnish

Namul is both the name for vegetables and the name of the technique used for cooking them. Basically, it is a way of seasoning vegetables that relies on the deep flavors of jang. Though this recipe is often made with dureup, or Japanese angelica, Broccolini, which shares some of the same mildly bitter flavor, works just as well. Blanching the vegetable softens the leaves and fibers, especially important later in the spring season.

Wash the Broccolini under cold running water. Trim the thick bottom stems and remove the leaves. Cut into 2¾-inch (7 cm) segments. (If there are flowers on the Broccolini, save them for later.)

Combine 8⅓ cups (2 L) water and the salt in a large pot and bring to a boil over high heat. Fill a large bowl with ice and water. Blanch the Broccolini in the boiling water for 2½ to 3 minutes, until bright green. Transfer to the ice bath to stop the cooking. Once cooled, drain and let dry.

In a large bowl, stir together the ganjang, 2¼ teaspoons of the sesame oil, and the ground sesame seeds. Add the blanched Broccolini and toss to combine. Finish with the whole sesame seeds, the remaining 1¾ teaspoons sesame oil, and the reserved Broccolini flowers, if you have them.

TIP: For a more robustly flavored namul, add 1 garlic clove, finely chopped; ¼ teaspoon finely chopped jalapeño or green Cheongyang chile; and 1 tablespoon finely chopped green onion; toss with the Broccolini and dressing.

HOBAK SEON 호박선
Layered Steamed Zucchini

SERVES 2

FOR THE BRINE

1 teaspoon hansik ganjang

1 teaspoon kosher salt

1 teaspoon honey

FOR THE ZUCCHINI

1 medium green zucchini, sliced lengthwise into thin ribbons on a mandoline

1 medium summer squash, sliced lengthwise into thin ribbons on a mandoline

2 teaspoons white balsamic vinegar

½ teaspoon extra-virgin olive oil (preferably a fruity, spicy variety), to finish

Steaming is a traditional cooking technique we use for many vegetables, from eggplant to zucchini to mushrooms. Such a simple method allows the natural flavors of the vegetable to emerge with minimal manipulation. With its delicate balance of saltiness plus gamchilmat, hansik ganjang allows the vegetable to reveal itself, or, actually, the best version of itself. This recipe is adapted from one I made for Buddhist nun Jeong Kwan. The challenge when she visits Mingles is to prepare a vegan menu that truly manifests simplicity while also, of course, delighting her. Here you'll use hansik ganjang both in the brine and as a finishing seasoning. The olive oil and white balsamic vinegar in the dish are influenced, obviously, by Italian cuisine. The interplay among the acid of the vinegar, the spiciness of the olive oil, and the saltiness of the ganjang forms a lovely canvas against which the subtly flavored zucchini stands out.

MAKE THE BRINE: In a small bowl, combine the ganjang, salt, honey, and ½ cup plus ⅓ cup (200 ml) room-temperature water and stir well. Place the zucchini and summer squash in a heatproof bowl, pour the brine over them, cover, and refrigerate for 1 to 2 hours.

COOK THE ZUCCHINI: Fill the bottom of a stacking steamer with water and bring to a boil. Set the bowl with the squash in it on the upper level of the steamer. Once steaming, cover and steam for 8 to 10 minutes. Remove the bowl from the steamer and place in the refrigerator, uncovered, for 15 minutes to cool.

To serve, remove the zucchini and summer squash from the brine, reserving the liquid. Stack one slice of green zucchini on one slice of summer squash, then carefully roll the stack into a tight spiral. Set the spiral on a plate and repeat with the remaining squash, placing the spirals one on top of another to form a loose pyramid as you work.

To finish, in a small bowl, mix 3 tablespoons (45 ml) of the reserved brine with the vinegar. Stir well and pour over the rolled squash. Drizzle with the olive oil and serve.

DUBU ENDIVE SALAD *with* SESAME GANJANG DRESSING

두부 엔다이브 샐러드와 참깨 간장 드레싱

SERVES 4

FOR THE VEGETABLE STOCK

½ medium onion, cut into ½-inch (1 cm) chunks

6 green onions, cut into ½-inch (1 cm) segments

½ daikon radish, peeled and cut into ½-inch (1 cm) chunks

5 dried pyogo (shiitake) mushrooms

FOR THE DUBU

1 tablespoon extra-virgin olive oil

1 (12-ounce/350 g) package medium-firm or firm dubu, cut into ½-inch (1.5 cm) pieces

2 tablespoons plus 1 teaspoon hansik ganjang

FOR THE SESAME GANJANG DRESSING

2 tablespoons brown rice vinegar

1 tablespoon extra-virgin olive oil

2¼ teaspoons toasted sesame oil

2 teaspoons hansik ganjang

1½ teaspoons honey

1 tablespoon sesame seeds, finely ground

Endive, more specifically Belgian endive, is not endemic to Korean cuisine. Yet it happens to be the perfect vehicle to showcase ganjang. Here you'll use ganjang in two ways to bring the ingredients of this simple salad into harmony. The sesame ganjang dressing serves to soften the bitterness of the endive. The flavor is nutty and just sweet enough to take the edge off. (It would make a great substitute for the balsamic vinegar and olive oil on a classic caprese salad, too.) Ganjang is also used as a brine for the dubu (bean curd—perhaps more familiar by its Japanese name, tofu), where it serves as a flavor enhancer, preventing the dubu from being overshadowed by the very assertive endive.

MAKE THE STOCK: In a large stockpot, combine the onion, green onions, daikon, mushrooms, and 6¼ cups (1.5 L) cold water and bring to a boil over medium heat. When the water begins to boil, skim off any impurities that rise to the surface. Reduce the heat to medium-low and simmer for 30 minutes, or until all the vegetables are cooked through. Remove from the heat and strain the stock into a container. Discard the solids.

MAKE THE DUBU: In a large nonstick skillet, heat the olive oil over medium heat until shimmering. Add the dubu pieces in a single layer and fry until golden brown, 4 to 5 minutes per side. Transfer the dubu to a plate, pat dry with a paper towel, and let cool slightly.

In a large deep bowl, combine 1½ cups (350 ml) of the vegetable stock with the ganjang and mix well. Add the dubu and set aside to marinate at room temperature for at least 1 hour or in the refrigerator for up to 1 day.

MEANWHILE, MAKE THE DRESSING: In a small bowl, whisk together the vinegar, olive oil, sesame oil, ganjang, honey, and sesame seeds until well blended; set aside.

When ready to serve, cut the dubu into bite-size pieces and sprinkle with half the lemon zest. Toss the endive leaves with 1½ tablespoons of the sesame ganjang dressing. Place the dubu in one layer on a plate, then shingle the endive leaves atop it.

TO SERVE

Zest of 1 lemon

2 medium Belgian endives, leaves trimmed, rinsed, and dried

Sprinkle with the remaining lemon zest and remaining sesame ganjang dressing to finish.

TIPS: Reserve the remaining vegetable stock for later use. Stock can be stored in an airtight container for up to 5 days in the refrigerator and up to 2 months in the freezer. If you have anchovy stock on hand, you can use it in place of the vegetable stock.

KONGGUKSU 콩국수
Chilled Soybean Noodle Soup

SERVES 2

¾ cup (120 g) dried yellow soybeans

2 cups (480 ml) unsweetened soy milk

2 teaspoons kosher salt

1½ teaspoons hansik ganjang

5½ ounces (160 g) somyeon (Korean wheat noodles)

¼ cucumber, thinly sliced

Pinch of black sesame seeds, ground

Every culture has—or should have—its own gazpacho, a cold soup for hot days to soothe the body and soul. In Korea, our version is kongguksu (*kong* means "soybeans"; *guksu* means "noodles"). Growing up, I loved this soup because eating it meant it was almost summer break, but I didn't love the flavor. It seemed bland. Over the years, I've come to appreciate the simplicity and the elegance of kongguksu. There are only three elements at play here: the soybean itself, the water, and the salt, in the form of hansik ganjang (itself a product of soybeans, water, and salt). Texturally silky with a creamy, hummus-like mouthfeel, the soup is both subtle and refreshing, with the wheat noodles imbuing an undercurrent of earthiness. Like a gazpacho, it goes well with cucumber and tomato or, if you're feeling adventurous, strawberries and blueberries. It does, however, take some planning, as you'll have to soak the soybeans a day in advance.

Put the soybeans in a large bowl, cover with cold water, and soak in the refrigerator for 1 day.

The next day, drain the soybeans and place in a large pot. Add 4¼ cups (1 L) water and bring to a boil over high heat. Reduce the heat to medium and simmer for 30 minutes, until the soybeans are soft but not mushy. Drain the cooked beans and transfer to a blender while still hot. Add the soy milk and ⅔ cup (150 ml) water and blend until smooth. Season the bean soup with the salt and ganjang.

Bring a large pot of water to a boil over high heat. Fill a large bowl with equal parts ice and cold water. Add the noodles to the boiling water and cook according to the package instructions, usually between 4½ and 5 minutes. Rinse the noodles well in the ice water several times until all the starch is removed. Drain the noodles.

To serve, divide the noodles evenly between two bowls. Slowly pour in the bean soup. Garnish with the cucumber and ground black sesame seeds.

TIP: Boiled barley or other grains can be used instead of noodles.

MIYEOK GUK 미역국
Seaweed Soup

SERVES 4

¾ ounce (20 g) dried miyeok or wakame seaweed

2 teaspoons kosher salt, plus more if needed

1½ teaspoons hansik ganjang, plus more if needed

4 ounces (115 g) brisket or short ribs

1½ teaspoons toasted sesame oil

2 garlic cloves, crushed

Freshly ground black pepper

3 cups (600 g) cooked rice, for serving

I don't know if I associate miyeok guk with comfort because it is traditionally eaten on birthdays as a way to honor our mothers, or whether mothers eat seaweed soup because it's so comforting in the first place. Thanks to the seaweed, this soup is certainly full of enough nutrients to nourish nursing mothers, especially important historically when other sources of protein were scarce. I grew up eating this brisket version in Seoul, but each region has its own variation. On Korea's east coast, they use dried pollack; in the northeast, potato; on Jeju Island, sea urchin; and in Chungcheong, wild sesame seed. No matter the variation, miyeok guk immediately imparts a sense of well-fed well-being.

Put the seaweed in a bowl and cover with room-temperature water. Set aside to soak for 30 minutes to 1 hour, until rehydrated. Drain and rinse the seaweed under running water, then drain again, squeezing it to remove the excess water. Cut it into 1-inch (2.5 cm) squares and place in a medium bowl. Add the salt and ganjang and mix well.

Meanwhile, put the brisket in a large bowl and cover with cold water. Place in the refrigerator and let soak for 30 minutes.

Drain the meat, then cut it into ¹⁄₁₀ by ¾ by ¾-inch (2.5 mm by 2 cm by 2 cm) strips and place in a heavy-bottomed pot. Add the seasoned seaweed and the sesame oil. Cook over medium-high heat, stirring continuously, for 5 minutes. Add 6¼ cups (1.5 L) water and the garlic and bring to a boil. Reduce the heat to medium-low and simmer, uncovered, for 1 hour, periodically skimming away any impurities that rise to the surface, until the seaweed turns smooth and the broth develops a rich seaweed flavor.

Season with pepper and additional ganjang or salt, if desired, and serve with the rice.

MANDU JEONGOL 만두전골
Korean Dumpling Hotpot

SERVES 2

FOR THE MANDU WRAPPER DOUGH

1¼ cups (150 g) bread flour

Pinch of kosher salt

FOR THE MANDU FILLING

3½ ounces (100 g) firm dubu, finely chopped

2 or 3 king oyster mushrooms, thinly sliced

⅓ zucchini, thinly sliced

⅓ medium onion, finely chopped

1 teaspoon neutral oil, such as grapeseed or canola

Kosher salt

7 ounces (200 g) minced pork, patted dry

2¼ teaspoons toasted sesame oil

2 teaspoons hansik ganjang

FOR THE HOTPOT

¼ onion, thinly sliced

¼ cup (30 g) thinly sliced stemmed pyogo (shiitake) mushrooms

¼ cup (30 g) sliced zucchini (⅓-inch-thick/ 0.75 cm half-moon slices)

5 cups (1.2 L) anchovy stock (see page 50)

2 tablespoons hansik ganjang

Many Koreans have memories of making dumpling soup with their mothers for Lunar New Year. I do, and now my kids do, too (although they will have memories of their dad in the kitchen as well). Across Asia, dumplings are symbolic of prosperity, which makes sense, since what are dumplings but little purses filled with precious cargo? Korean dumplings, or mandu, are unique because the filling has an unusually high ratio of dubu and vegetables to meat. This might be a result of Koreans' economic austerity, but the effect is a light dumpling that doesn't leave you uncomfortably stuffed.

When making mandu for this soup, use a slightly thicker dumpling wrapper so the dumplings don't burst open while cooking. "Soup" isn't quite the right word for this dish. Jeongol is more like a hotpot in which the dumplings are cooked tableside in a light hansik ganjang–flavored broth. Most families, mine included, have a gaeseu-beoneo (gas burner) on which we make our jeongol (and bulgogi and samgyeopsal). This stovetop grill turns the cooking itself into an interactive experience and allows for infinite personalization. Buddhist nun Jeong Kwan, for instance, makes her mandu jeongol with pyogo (shiitake) mushrooms. My parents often put in chicken or shrimp in addition to pork. I like seafood, too, with extra napa cabbage in the broth. What you put in your mandu or your broth is up to you, though I recommend keeping a high ratio of dubu and vegetables to meat.

MAKE THE DOUGH: In a bowl, knead together the flour, salt, and ¼ cup (60 ml) water until a smooth dough forms. Wrap the dough in plastic wrap and let rest in the refrigerator for at least 1 hour and up to overnight.

MEANWHILE, MAKE THE MANDU FILLING: Blot the dubu with a paper towel to remove excess moisture; set aside.

In a large pan, heat the neutral oil over low heat until shimmering. Add the mushroom, zucchini, and onions and sweat for about 10 minutes, until the moisture has been removed. Lightly season with salt, then transfer the vegetables to a tray and let cool.

In a medium bowl, stir together the cooled vegetables, pork, dubu, sesame oil, and ganjang and set aside.

ingredients continue

recipe continues

1 garlic clove, minced

4 green onions, thinly sliced on the diagonal

1 napa cabbage leaf, cut into 1-inch-wide (2.5 cm) strips

½ red chile, thinly sliced on the diagonal

MAKE THE DUMPLINGS: To form the wrappers, divide the dough into 10 equal portions, each about the size of a golf ball. Use a rolling pin to roll out each piece of dough into a 4-inch (10 cm) round, 1 millimeter thick. (If you'd like, you can use either a cookie cutter or, very carefully, a knife.) Freeze any remaining dough for later use.

Portion out about 2½ tablespoons of the filling per wrapper. Spread a little water over the edge of half the wrapper, fold it in half, and press the edges firmly to seal, forming a half-moon. (Make sure air does not go inside the dumpling when you fold it.) Bring the pointed ends of the half-moon together and press firmly to seal; set the dumpling on a plate and repeat to fill the remaining wrappers.

MAKE THE HOTPOT: Spread the onion, mushrooms, and zucchini over the bottom of a large, wide pot. Place the dumplings atop the vegetables, then add the stock, ganjang, and garlic. Bring the stock to a boil over high heat, then immediately reduce the heat to medium and simmer for 5 minutes. Add the green onions, cabbage, and chile and simmer for 5 minutes more. Serve immediately.

TAGLIATELLE *with* GANJANG RAGÙ

간장 라구 탈리아텔레

SERVES 2

FOR THE GANJANG RAGÙ

3½ tablespoons (50 ml) light mat-ganjang (see page 53)

1½ tablespoons yangjo doenjang

2 teaspoons canola oil

1 garlic clove, chopped

1 green onion, white part only, chopped

1 small white onion, finely diced

2 or 3 medium button mushrooms, finely diced

3 or 4 celery stalks, finely diced

½ pound (250 g) ground beef, patted dry

FOR THE TAGLIATELLE

7 ounces (200 g) tagliatelle

Kosher salt

¾ cup (180 ml) heavy cream

1 tablespoon plus 1 teaspoon grated Grana Padano cheese, plus more for serving

Pinch of freshly ground black pepper, for garnish

2 teaspoons chopped fresh parsley, for garnish

Ganjang ragù is the most versatile sauce. It combines everything I love about ragù—or in this case, a tomato-free ragù bianco—with everything I love about ganjang. The deep, comforting flavors of the slowly simmered meat are underscored by the even deeper tones of ganjang. (The ganjang replaces the higher-acid white wine often used in Bolognese sauce.) Seen through the lens of hansik, this ragù is a variant of a traditional bibimbap sauce, which is where this idea began. Using ganjang instead of gochujang, however, allows the sauce to pair well with dairy, thus opening up an entire world of mostly Western pairings. This ragù is a perfect Sunday sauce served over pasta. I usually double or even triple the recipe; I store some in the fridge, where it will keep for 3 to 5 days, and freeze the rest for up to 3 months.

MAKE THE RAGÙ: In a small bowl, mix together the mat-ganjang, doenjang, and ¼ cup (60 ml) water. Set aside.

In a large heavy-bottomed pot, heat the canola oil over medium heat until shimmering. Add the garlic and green onion and cook until softened but not browned. Add the white onion, mushrooms, and celery, in that order; reduce the heat to low and sauté until lightly browned, about 10 minutes. Add the ground beef and cook, stirring, until browned, about 10 minutes. Add the mat-ganjang mixture and simmer for 15 to 20 minutes.

MAKE THE TAGLIATELLE: Bring a large pot of well-salted water to a boil over high heat. Add the pasta and cook according to the package directions (tagliatelle usually takes between 4 and 6 minutes to cook, depending on the brand).

Meanwhile, pour the cream into the ragù and mix well to thicken.

Drain the pasta well, then add it to the pot with the ragù and toss to coat. Add the Grana Padano and mix once more. Serve the tagliatelle with the pepper, parsley, and extra cheese sprinkled on top.

Nine Ways to Use Ganjang Ragù

1. Pour ½ cup (120 g) of the ragù over rice and add vegetables to make a mild **bibimbap**.

2. Spread 2 tablespoons of the ragù atop a thick slice of toasted sourdough bread. Top with a sunny-side-up egg for a perfect **breakfast toast**.

3. To make a **quesadilla**, spread ¼ cup (60 g) of the ragù and ¼ cup (45 g) shredded Monterey Jack or cheddar cheese over a tortilla. Set the tortilla in a skillet over low heat and cover. Cook until the cheese has melted, then fold the tortilla in half, press firmly with a spatula, and serve.

4. Combine the ragù with tomato sauce in a 1:1 ratio and use as a substitute for your regular pizza sauce to make **bulgogi pizza**.

5. Use the ragù as a substitute for Bolognese sauce when making **lasagna**.

6. Add ½ cup (90 g) cooked kidney beans, ¼ cup (30 g) cooked green peas, ½ cup (80 g) cooked corn kernels, and 1 tablespoon coarsely ground gochugaru to 1 cup (240 g) ragù to turn it into a **chili con carne**.

7. When making **shepherd's pie**, substitute the ragù for the ground beef called for in the recipe.

8. Use the ragù instead of Mornay sauce as a base for **mac and cheese**.

9. Combine equal parts ragù, dubu, and vegetables and use as a filling for either **mandu** or **spring rolls**.

JAPCHAE 잡채
Glass Noodles with Mixed Vegetables

SERVES 2

3½ ounces (100 g) dried glass noodles

¼ cup (60 ml) yangjo ganjang

1 tablespoon sugar

1 teaspoon toasted sesame oil

1 garlic clove, minced

2 tablespoons neutral oil, such as grapeseed or canola

¼ medium onion, thinly sliced (see Tip)

½ teaspoon kosher salt

2 pyogo (shiitake) mushrooms, stemmed and thinly sliced

¼ bell pepper, seeded and thinly sliced

½ medium carrot, thinly sliced

About 10 chives, cut into 1¼-inch-long (3 cm) segments

Pinch of sesame seeds

TIP: Using a spiralizer to thinly slice the vegetables will save you lots of time. You can also use a mandoline to cut the carrots into sheets before thinly slicing into strips.

A simple dish that can be time-consuming to make, homemade japchae isn't everyday food in Korea. It is, however, omnipresent for birthdays, New Year celebrations, anniversaries, and holidays. When it was first made in the seventeenth century during the Joseon dynasty, japchae was simply a celebration of finely cut vegetables. It took until the twentieth century, and the introduction of sweet potato starch noodles (or glass noodles), for its modern form to take shape. The beauty of japchae is in the mingling of the vegetables. When equally cut, they tangle and furrow through the noodles so each bite is perfectly harmonious.

Submerge the noodles in a bowl of hot water (85° to 105°F/30° to 40°C) and soak for 30 minutes to 1 hour.

Meanwhile, in a small bowl, mix the ganjang, sugar, sesame oil, and garlic; set aside.

In a skillet, heat ½ tablespoon of the neutral oil over medium heat until shimmering. Add the onion and salt and cook until golden and soft, a minute or two. Transfer the onion to a tray near the stove. Add another ½ tablespoon of the neutral oil to the pan and heat until shimmering. Add the mushrooms and cook for 1 minute, then transfer to the tray. Add another ½ tablespoon of the oil and the bell pepper to the pan and cook for 1 minute, then transfer to the tray. Add the remaining ½ tablespoon of the oil and the carrot to the pan and cook until softened, about 2 minutes, then transfer to the tray. Spread the vegetables into a single layer to cool.

While the vegetables cool, bring 10 cups (2.5 L) water to a boil in a large pot. Drain the glass noodles, add them to the boiling water, and cook for 3 minutes, then drain and quickly rinse with cold water. Drain once more and transfer to a medium bowl.

Add the ganjang mixture to the bowl and mix until the noodles are coated. Transfer the noodles to a large pan, add the vegetables, and toss to combine. Cook over medium heat for 2 to 3 minutes, until they are piping hot. Transfer to a serving platter, top with the chives and sesame seeds, and serve.

ASPARAGUS BIBIMBAP

아스파라거스 비빔밥

SERVES 2

FOR THE BIBIM GANJANG SAUCE

⅓ green onion, finely chopped

2 garlic cloves, finely chopped

2 tablespoons hansik ganjang

1 tablespoon toasted sesame oil

1½ teaspoons ground sesame seeds

1½ teaspoons finely chopped seeded red chile

½ teaspoon finely chopped seeded green Cheongyang chile or jalapeño

FOR THE ASPARAGUS

Kosher salt

15 to 20 pencil asparagus stalks

2 to 3 white asparagus stalks, if available

1½ cups (300 g) cooked rice, for serving

Edible flowers, such as calendula (optional)

Vegetables, or namul, are what kept Koreans alive for many years when animal protein was scarce and we had to forage for food (long before foraging was cool). The result is that hansik is full of nuanced and skilled preparations for cooking vegetables. We divide namul preparations into saengchae (raw vegetables) and sukchae (blanched vegetables). Often sukchae consist of leafy greens, such as dureup (Japanese angelica shoots) and minari (water dropwort), for which blanching softens some of the bitter flavor. The same technique works with asparagus.

MAKE THE SAUCE: In a small bowl, whisk together the green onion, garlic, ganjang, sesame oil, sesame seeds, and red and green chiles. Set aside.

MAKE THE ASPARAGUS: Bring a pot of salted water to a boil. Fill a large bowl with equal parts ice and cold water. Blanch the pencil asparagus in the boiling water for 2 to 3 minutes, then transfer to the ice bath to stop the cooking. Trim the bottoms of the stalks and cut into 1¼- to 1½-inch (3 to 4 cm) pieces.

Trim the white asparagus (if using) and thinly slice them lengthwise on a mandoline or with a vegetable peeler.

In a large bowl, combine half the sauce and the green asparagus and toss to coat. Serve the sauced asparagus atop bowls of rice, alongside the white asparagus (if using) and garnished with flowers, if desired, with the remaining sauce on the side.

GANJANG BEOSEOT TTEOKBOKKI

간장 버섯 떡볶이

Ganjang Tteokbokki with Mushrooms

SERVES 2

2 cups (300 g) chopped
fresh or thawed frozen
rice tteok (bite-size pieces)

⅓ cup (80 ml) dark
mat-ganjang (see page 53)

1 garlic clove, minced

2 tablespoons canola oil

½ onion, cut into 1-inch-
thick (2.5 cm) slices

5 medium button
mushrooms, cleaned
and halved or quartered

2 pyogo (shiitake)
mushrooms, cleaned
and quartered

½ bunch (40 g) enoki
mushrooms, cleaned and
bottom portions removed

2 green onions, trimmed
and cut into ¼-inch (6 mm)
segments

Sesame seeds, for garnish

1 teaspoon toasted
sesame oil

In Korea, where rice is a precious food, if you are going to turn it into a secondary product, the result had better justify the effort. Thankfully, tteok does just that. A luxurious, spongy, and versatile cylindrical rice cake, tteok can be eaten both sweet and savory. I love tteok because it blends so easily with other ingredients.

Though tteokbokki is commonly tossed with gochujang (which is extremely delicious), this traditional recipe, made with ganjang, brings out the sweetness of the tteok as well as the deep flavor of the ganjang. It's a vegan preparation where both the mushrooms and the ganjang supercharge the dish with an earthy flavor.

NOTE: Though fresh tteokbokki is ideal, it can be difficult to find. Frozen tteok is, however, plentiful. Presoaking the thawed tteokbokki isn't absolutely necessary, but it does improve the chewiness and texture.

Put the tteok in a bowl and cover with cold water. Soak for 30 minutes, then drain well and set aside.

In a small bowl, mix together the mat-ganjang, garlic, and 1 cup (240 ml) water; set aside.

In a cast-iron skillet, heat the canola oil over medium heat until shimmering. Add the onion, button mushrooms, and pyogo mushrooms and cook until golden brown, about 2 minutes. Add the ganjang mixture and the tteok to the pan and bring the mixture to a boil. Reduce the heat to low and simmer for 10 minutes, allowing the sauce to reduce. Add the enoki mushrooms and the green onions and cook for 1 minute.

To serve, divide the tteokbokki evenly between two plates, garnish with sesame seeds, and finish by drizzling the sesame oil over the top.

EO-MANDU 어만두
Fish Dumpling

SERVES 4

2 fillets red mullet or
other fatty white-fleshed
fish (320 g)

½ teaspoon kosher salt

FOR THE MANDU FILLING

2 ounces (50 g) firm dubu

1 tablespoon neutral oil,
such as canola or vegetable
oil

⅓ cup (50 g) finely diced
zucchini

⅔ cup (50 g) finely diced
king oyster mushroom

¼ onion, finely diced

⅓ cup (50 g) finely diced
fennel bulb

⅛ teaspoon kosher salt

1 teaspoon hansik ganjang

TO FINISH

½ cup plus 2 tablespoons
(140 ml) light mat-ganjang
(see page 53)

¼ cup (60 ml) brown rice
vinegar

1 green onion, sliced into
thin strips, for garnish

This recipe is in the tradition of Joseon dynasty royal court cuisine, an elaborate codified way of eating that stretched from the beginning of the dynasty (1392) to its end (1910) and was heavily influenced by seasonal and religious rites. Fish mandu or dumplings made using small filefish are often eaten during the summer. The fish in fish mandu—in this case, red mullet—doesn't refer to the filling but to the wrapper. The filling is the traditional dubu-and-vegetable mixture. The process of making mandu is quite straightforward. The only thing you'll need is plenty of time to allow the fish to marinate and the filling to cool.

Cut each fillet in half crosswise, then carefully butterfly each portion. Sprinkle the salt evenly over both sides of the fish and set aside.

MAKE THE FILLING: Mash the dubu with the side of a knife blade, then blot it with a paper towel to remove any excess moisture.

In a large skillet, heat the oil over high heat until shimmering. Add the zucchini, mushroom, onion, fennel, and salt and cook, stirring occasionally, until softened, about 10 minutes. Transfer the vegetables to a paper towel–lined tray to cool.

In a large bowl, mix together the vegetables, dubu, and ganjang. Cover and refrigerate until ready to use.

To assemble the mandu, lay the butterflied fish flat on a work surface. Divide the filling into 4 equal portions and spread one portion over one side of each piece of fish, then carefully fold the other side over the filling. Use a knife to push any excess filling inside.

In a heatproof bowl large enough to hold the fish, mix together the mat-ganjang and vinegar. Gently place the fish mandu in the mixture. Fill the bottom of a stacking steamer with water and bring to a boil. Set the bowl with the fish mandu in it on the upper level of the steamer. Cover and steam for 6 to 8 minutes, until the fish is opaque and fully cooked.

To serve, strain any leftover ganjang-vinegar sauce and divide it among four shallow bowls or plates. Place a fish mandu atop the sauce in each bowl and garnish with the green onion.

HAEMUL PAJEON 해물파전
Seafood Scallion Pancake

SERVES 2

1 cup (120 g) all-purpose flour

1 tablespoon hansik ganjang

¾ teaspoon kosher salt

Pinch of freshly ground black pepper

1 (3½-ounce/100 g) calamari, cleaned and cut into small chunks

8 jumbo shrimp (100 g), peeled, deveined, and cut into chunks

½ zucchini, diced

5 or 6 green onions, cut into 1-inch (2.5 cm) segments

6 to 7 tablespoons (90 to 105 ml) neutral oil, such as grapeseed or canola

1 ounce (30 g) onion jangajji (see page 60), thinly sliced

When I was a boy hooked on cooking shows, making dinner for my parents was my greatest joy. When they liked it, I was even happier. Pajeon (scallion pancake) was an easy win. Why? They are incredibly easy to make, and everybody loves a pajeon. It has the crispiness of a pizza but the give of a pancake. The base ingredients are so simple, you most likely have them on hand already. Plus, pajeon are easy to customize. You can fill them with kimchi, like my dad loved to do, or with calamari and shrimp, as my mom preferred. However you fill them, pajeon are perhaps best enjoyed with a glass of makgeolli or soju.

Sift the flour into a large bowl, then add ¾ cup (180 ml) cold water. Whisk until no lumps remain, then add the ganjang, salt, and pepper, whisking until incorporated. Cover and refrigerate until ready to use.

When you're ready to cook, add the calamari, shrimp, zucchini, and green onions to the bowl with the batter and stir to coat.

In a 12-inch (30 cm) skillet, heat 2 tablespoons of the oil over medium heat until it begins to smoke. Pour half the batter into the pan. Once the edge of the pancake begins to fry, reduce the heat to medium and cook until the bottom of the pancake is browned and cooked evenly, about 5 minutes. Slide the pancake onto a plate and add another 1 to 1½ tablespoons of the oil. Gently flip the pancake back into the pan and cook, pressing it down so the uncooked side also becomes crunchy, for 3 minutes. Transfer the pancake to a paper towel–lined plate to drain. Repeat with the remaining batter.

Serve piping hot, with a side of onion jangajji.

GANJANG SAEWOO JANG 간장 새우장
Ganjang-Marinated Shrimp

SERVES 2

FOR THE GANJANG MARINADE

½ cup plus 2 tablespoons (140 ml) light mat-ganjang (see page 53)

½ teaspoon whole black peppercorns

⅛ small onion, thinly sliced

1 green onion, white part only, thinly sliced

¼ green Cheongyang chile or jalapeño, coarsely chopped

¼-inch (6 mm) piece fresh ginger, peeled and chopped (optional)

1 large garlic clove, chopped

1 teaspoon hansik ganjang

FOR THE SHRIMP

10 jumbo shrimp or Mediterranean red shrimp, deveined

2 garlic cloves, thinly sliced

1 green Cheongyang chile or jalapeño, thinly sliced

TO SERVE

½ red chile, thinly sliced

½ green onion, white part only, thinly sliced

1½ cups (300 g) cooked rice

1 teaspoon toasted sesame oil

This dish hails from Taean County, famous for its pristine waters, Technicolor sunsets, and beautiful mud flats. The area is almost as well-known for ganjang-gejang, sweet blue she-crab marinated with ganjang. The crabs are caught in springtime and flash-frozen to last the year. Ganjang-gejang is served at beachside restaurants throughout the area, the most famous of which is Hwa Hae Dang (Flower Crab House). The crab's flesh, complemented with bright orange roe, is accented by the salt of the ganjang but still preserves its silken texture and innate sweetness. If you can get blue crab, do. But you can achieve a similarly delicious play of texture and flavor with shrimp.

The longer the shrimp stays in the mat-ganjang mixture, the saltier it becomes. Two days in ganjang achieves the perfect balance, infusing the shrimp with the complex flavors of the marinade without overpowering its delicacy. As with all preparations relying on so few elements, freshness and high-quality ingredients, especially the shrimp, are key.

MAKE THE MARINADE: In a medium pot, combine the mat-ganjang, peppercorns, onion, green onion, chile, ginger, garlic, and 1 cup (240 ml) water and bring to a simmer over medium heat. Cook for 5 minutes, then remove from the heat, cover with a lid, and let cool to room temperature. (The longer it sits, the more strongly flavored the marinade will be.) Strain the marinade into a nonreactive container, discarding the solids, then stir in the ganjang.

MAKE THE SHRIMP: Rinse the shrimp well in cold water. Add the shrimp, garlic, and green chile to the container with the marinade, cover, and refrigerate for 2 to 5 days.

Evenly divide the shrimp between two plates and pour ¼ cup (60 ml) of the marinade over them. Sprinkle the red chile and green onion over the top. Serve with the rice, drizzled with the sesame oil. (Note: Remove the heads before you eat.)

GODEUNG-EO JORIM 간장 고등어 조림
Ganjang-Braised Mackerel

SERVES 2

FOR THE GANJANG SAUCE

3½ tablespoons (55 ml) light mat-ganjang (see page 53)

1½ tablespoons gochugaru

2 teaspoons hansik ganjang

½ teaspoon toasted sesame oil

2 garlic cloves, minced

Pinch of whole black peppercorns

FOR THE FISH

⅙ medium daikon radish, peeled and cut into ½-inch-thick (1 cm) slices

2 (3-ounce/90 g) fillets fresh mackerel or Spanish mackerel, rinsed and patted dry

¼ medium onion, thinly sliced (¼-inch/6 mm slices)

1 green onion, white part only, cut into ½-inch (1 cm) segments

½ green Cheongyang chile or jalapeño, thinly sliced (¹⁄₁₆-inch/2 mm slices)

Jorim and jjim are close cousins. Both are methods of braising a protein, often in jang. The focus of a jorim is to render the meat tender; the point of a jjim is to infuse the protein with the delicious braising liquid. In some ways, therefore, jang plays an even more important role in jorim than in jjim. This recipe is more of a technique than a recipe per se. I use mackerel, a strongly flavored fatty fish, but feel free to use whatever fish is local. (The same goes for the vegetables, though braising works better with fleshy vegetables like radishes and onions than with leafy ones—the exception being a tangy cabbage kimchi, which goes with everything, always.) Braising the fish under the cover of parchment paper deeply infuses the flavored jang into the already soft fish, supercharging the fish with the delicately spiced ganjang sauce.

MAKE THE SAUCE: In a small bowl, mix together the mat-ganjang, gochugaru, hansik ganjang, sesame oil, garlic, peppercorns, and ½ cup plus ⅓ cup (200 ml) water and set aside.

MAKE THE FISH: Tile the daikon slices over the bottom of a flat, wide pot, then top with the fish fillets and onion. Pour the ganjang sauce over the fish until the fillets are covered in the sauce. Place a piece of parchment paper over the fish and set the pot over medium heat. When the liquid begins to boil, reduce the heat to maintain a simmer and cook for 15 to 20 minutes, lifting up the paper to baste the vegetables and fish with the liquid every 5 minutes. When the fish is opaque and nearly fully cooked, add the green onion and chile. Simmer for 1 minute more, then serve immediately.

GALBIJJIM 갈비찜
Braised Short Ribs

SERVES 4

3 cups (720 ml) dark mat-ganjang (see page 53)

6 garlic cloves, peeled

1 (½-inch/1 cm) knob fresh ginger, peeled

½ Korean (Asian) pear, peeled and cored

4½ pounds (2 kg) bone-in beef short ribs, cut into 1½-inch (4 cm) chunks

15 raw chestnuts, peeled and soaked in water

⅓ medium daikon radish, peeled and cut into 1-inch (2.5 cm) cubes

1 large carrot, cut into 1-inch (2.5 cm) cubes

5 medium pyogo (shiitake) mushrooms, cleaned, trimmed, and quartered

2 dried red chiles

5 dried jujubes

1 egg, separated

Neutral oil, such as grapeseed or canola, for the pan

Galbi means "rib" in Korean, and *jjim* means something between braising and steaming, so *galbijjim* is "braised rib." Though you can make galbi with pork short ribs, we use beef short ribs in this recipe. And ganjang is by far the best liquid to make galbijjim. Gochujang is so strong, it fundamentally alters whatever is being braised. Doenjang, meanwhile, has a tendency to deeply color the braise and loses its nutrients when braised too long. Succulent and tender when left alone long enough in its braise, beef galbi demands time, which ganjang can withstand. (If you're braising chicken or pork, both of which cook faster, gochujang or doenjang can work.)

Galbijjim is delicious all year round, but for me it is always associated with chestnut season in Korea, which lasts from mid-autumn to winter. Our chestnuts tend to be a little larger and less sweet than the American variety (though even American chestnuts add a lovely smokiness to the meal). A good galbijjim is like coq au vin, but with beef. Each element, from the mushrooms to the chestnuts to the beef itself, retains its individual identity but works in harmony with its compatriots. Though it is by no means necessary, if you're making galbijjim for a special occasion, finish it with jidan, an egg garnish similar to a segregated omelet from the pantheon of royal cuisine, which provides harmonious color as well as flavor.

In a food processor, combine the mat-ganjang, garlic, ginger, and pear and pulse to incorporate.

Bring a large pot of water to a boil. Blanch the short ribs in the boiling water for 1 minute, then carefully remove them and set aside. Empty the pot then add 6⅔ cups (1.6 L) water, the mat-ganjang mixture, and the blanched ribs. Bring the liquid to a boil over medium heat, then reduce the heat to low and simmer for 1 hour, ensuring that the meat is entirely covered in the sauce. Add the chestnuts, daikon, carrot, mushrooms, chiles, and jujubes and cook for 40 minutes more, until the vegetables are tender and the meat falls off the bone. Remove from the heat, cover, and let sit for 10 minutes.

Meanwhile, beat the egg white and yolk in separate small bowls. In a lightly oiled nonstick pan, cook the yolk over medium-low heat until just set but not colored, then flip and cook for 30 seconds

more. Transfer the cooked yolk to a plate and repeat the process with the egg white. Let the cooked yolk and white cool, then cut both into 1-inch (2.5 cm) diamonds.

Serve the galbi family-style on a large platter, topped with the egg strips.

TIP: Galbi is even better the day after it's made, when the meat and liquid have had a chance to settle. To reheat the galbijjim, skim the solid fat from the top of the liquid and heat the liquid and the meat together.

LA GALBI GUI LA 갈비구이
LA-Style Grilled Short Ribs

SERVES 4

FOR THE GALBI GANJANG MARINADE

1 cup (240 ml) dark mat-ganjang (see page 53)

¼ Korean (Asian) pear, cored

¼ onion, coarsely chopped

3 garlic cloves, minced

¼-inch (6 mm) piece fresh ginger, coarsely chopped

2 tablespoons plus ¾ teaspoon neutral oil, such as grapeseed or canola

2 tablespoons plus ¾ teaspoon toasted sesame oil

1½ tablespoons honey or pure maple syrup

1½ teaspoons kosher salt

Pinch of freshly ground black pepper

2 pounds (1 kg) LA-cut short ribs, ½ inch (1 cm) thick

1 small onion, thinly sliced

3 green onions, white parts only, thinly sliced

4 cups (800 g) cooked rice

2 tablespoons plus 1 teaspoon toasted sesame oil

1 teaspoon yangjo ganjang

⅔ cup (8 g) fresh cilantro leaves, for garnish

Galbi (beef short rib) is to beef what samgyeopsal (pork belly) is to pork: the most flavorful, most beloved, most prized cut of the animal. The balance between fat and meat makes short ribs the ideal vehicle for a marinade and thus for grilling—in other words, the ideal platform to show how ganjang can enrich the flavors of meat. The marinade does double duty. While the mat-ganjang gets to work, enzymes from the Korean pear work to break down the peptides of the protein, resulting in tender meat. Whereas in Korea we use short ribs cut along the bone, in the United States it's more common to find so-called LA galbi, cut across the bone. Though the history is debated, most agree this style began with Korean immigrants in Los Angeles adapting to the American penchant for rib eye. Eventually, given the two-way flow of the diaspora, this style became popular in Korea, too.

MAKE THE MARINADE: In a blender, combine the mat-ganjang, pear, onion, garlic, ginger, neutral oil, sesame oil, honey, salt, pepper, and ⅓ cup plus 1 tablespoon (100 ml) water and blend until smooth.

Place the ribs in a large airtight container, pour in the marinade, and set aside to marinate at room temperature for at least 1 hour and up to overnight.

Meanwhile, soak the onion and the green onions in a bowl of ice water for 30 minutes to mellow out the flavor. Drain and set aside.

Prepare a charcoal or barbecue grill for high heat, or heat a large skillet over high heat. Grill the short ribs, turning them often so the marinade does not burn, until the sauce is slightly caramelized and the meat is cooked medium-well, 3 to 5 minutes. Transfer the meat to a platter and let rest until it has cooled a bit, then cut it into bite-size pieces.

While the meat is resting, in a medium bowl, combine the rice, sesame oil, and ganjang and toss well.

To serve, put some seasoned rice on each plate and place some of the onions beside it. Place the sliced galbi next to the rice and garnish with the cilantro.

TTEOKGALBI 떡갈비
Short Rib Burgers

SERVES 2

FOR THE KIMCHI-ROLLED RICE

1 cup (200 g) cooked rice

2 teaspoons toasted sesame oil

½ teaspoon hansik ganjang

12 leaves white kimchi, cut into 3½-inch (9 cm) squares, using mainly leafy parts

FOR THE PATTIES

14 ounces (400 g) boneless short ribs, coarsely ground

⅓ cup (80 ml) dark mat-ganjang (see page 53)

¼ onion, coarsely chopped

1 green onion, white part only, coarsely chopped

2 garlic cloves, minced

¾ teaspoon honey or pure maple syrup

FOR THE HERB GARNISH

½ teaspoon hansik ganjang

½ teaspoon toasted sesame oil

½ teaspoon brown rice vinegar

¼ cup (5 g) fresh chervil leaves

Tteokgalbi means "rice cake ribs" (*tteok* is "rice cake"; *galbi* is "short ribs"), but the rice is present in name only. In this dish, the meat itself is formed into patties much like rice can be. This is an old dish from the Joseon dynasty, when it was called *no-galbi*, or "elder ribs." Like the Awadhi kebabs from Lucknow, this soft meat patty was designed for the toothless. Traditionally tteokgalbi is served as part of bansang; that is, surrounded by an array of banchan and rice. But in this preparation, I've combined many of those elements into one dish you can eat either with a knife and fork (or chopsticks) or, if you like, on a bun. It's not quite a hamburger. It's better.

Preheat the oven to 400°F (200°C).

MAKE THE RICE: In a medium bowl, mix together the rice, sesame oil, and ganjang until well coated. Divide the rice into 12 mounds of about 1 tablespoon each. Place a mound of rice close to the edge of a square of white kimchi, then roll the kimchi around the rice to enclose it. Place on a baking sheet and repeat with the remaining rice; set the kimchi-rolled rice aside at room temperature.

MAKE THE PATTIES: In a large bowl, mix together the ground beef, mat-ganjang, onion, green onion, garlic, and honey to combine. Form the meat mixture into 4 oval-shaped patties, 2¾ to 3 inches (6.75 to 7.5 cm) in diameter.

When ready to cook, heat a cast-iron skillet over high heat or preheat a charcoal grill to high. Place the patties on the hot surface and cook, making sure to turn them every 30 to 60 seconds, for a total of 6 to 7 minutes. If the exteriors of the patties are charred but the insides are not quite done, transfer the pan to the oven and cook for 5 minutes, until completely cooked inside.

MAKE THE HERB GARNISH: In a bowl, mix together the ganjang, sesame oil, and vinegar to form a dressing.

Divide the tteokgalbi between two plates and put the kimchi-rolled rice alongside. Just before serving, toss the chervil in the dressing and serve immediately, alongside the tteokgalbi and kimchi-rolled rice.

YAKBAP 약밥
Sweet Sticky Rice Cake

SERVES 4

1¼ cups (250 g) uncooked glutinous rice

2 or 3 dried jujubes

¼ cup (25 g) walnut halves

1 tablespoon pine nuts

½ cup packed (100 g) brown sugar

2 tablespoons yangjo ganjang

1½ tablespoons honey

1½ tablespoons toasted sesame oil, plus more for the pan

8 raw chestnuts, peeled and quartered

Traditionally Koreans eat yakbap, a sweetened spiced sticky rice cake, on Jeongwol Daeboreum, a festival in January that celebrates the first full moon of the new year. I, on the other hand, eat yakbap any chance I get. To me, it's the perfect snack, a sweet (but not super sweet) rice that you don't need to heat up. Make it with glutinous rice (bap); *yak* means "medicine" and refers to honey, traditionally thought of as part of the pharmacopoeia. When I'm traveling or don't have time for a full meal, I'll grab some yakbap and shove it in my pocket to eat later like the world's most delicious rice-based protein bar. (In a well-sealed container, yakbap keeps for 3 days.)

Preheat the oven to 250°F (120°C).

Rinse the glutinous rice three times in cold water, then place in a bowl of fresh cold water and refrigerate for 6 hours.

Trim the tops and bottoms of the jujubes. Using a sharp knife, make an incision from the top to the bottom of the jujube flesh and remove the seed. You should be left with a sheet of seedless jujube; repeat with each jujube. Using a rolling pin, press the jujube sheets until they are flat and very thin. Roll each sheet into a tight spiral, then thinly slice each roll crosswise. Place the jujube strips on a baking sheet, then dry in the oven with the door slightly open for 30 minutes.

Drain the rice and set aside.

In a dry pan, lightly toast the walnuts over medium heat, stirring continuously, until the nuts are fragrant, about 3 minutes. Remove the walnuts from the pan and let cool slightly. Meanwhile, add the pine nuts to the pan and toast over low heat, stirring, for about 3 minutes. Remove from the heat. Coarsely chop the toasted walnuts. Reserve 10 or so pine nuts for garnish.

In a small bowl, combine the brown sugar, ganjang, honey, sesame oil, and ⅓ cup plus 1 tablespoon (100 ml) water and mix until the sugar has completely dissolved.

Coat a straight-sided 9-inch (23 cm) round pan with a thin layer of sesame oil. In a pressure cooker, mix together the soaked rice, chestnuts, toasted pine nuts, and ganjang mixture. If you are using

an electric pressure cooker, cook the rice using the multigrain rice function. If using a gas-powered pressure cooker, cook on the high-heat setting until the vent rings, then reduce the heat to low and cook for 13 minutes more; remove from the heat and let rest for 15 minutes. When the rice is done, transfer it to a bowl and mix in the chopped toasted walnuts, then, while it is still warm, press the rice mixture into the prepared pan and let cool completely.

To serve, remove the yakbap from the pan and cut it into wedges. Top each with some of the jujube strips and reserved pine nuts.

GANJANG GRANOLA YOGURT

간장 그래놀라와 요거트

SERVES 4

¼ cup (60 ml) pure maple syrup or honey

3 tablespoons (45 ml) extra-virgin olive oil

1 tablespoon plus 1 teaspoon yangjo ganjang

1⅓ cups (150 g) rolled oats

¼ cup (50 g) almond slices

¼ cup (25 g) pecans or walnuts, quartered

¼ cup (50 g) hulled pumpkin seeds (pepitas)

1 egg white

¼ cup (50 g) dried cranberries

2 cups (480 g) plain whole-milk yogurt

⅔ cup (40 g) fresh blueberries

1 white peach, pitted and cubed

4 mint sprigs, for garnish (optional)

Granola is not part of the hansik breakfast, and yet, with its endless variations and add-ins, I find it irresistible. The truth is that this ganjang granola got its start at the end of a meal, as part of a "jang trio" at Mingles that also included the Doenjang Vanilla Crème Brûlée on page 147 and a gochujang powder. One day when I came into the restaurant in the morning to find some leftover granola, I added it to my yogurt and, well, the result became my go-to breakfast.

What I particularly like about this recipe is how the egg white acts as a binding agent without adding too much sweetness. (Some American granolas taste like candy to me.) The ganjang provides a slightly salted caramelly taste without pumping the mixture with sugar. As for the accoutrements—the nuts, the seeds, the fruit—personalize as you see fit. The core of this recipe is the mixture of the olive oil, maple syrup, ganjang, and egg white. Make a double or even triple batch of the recipe and keep some in the freezer for up to 6 months.

Preheat the oven to 300°F (150°C).

In a small bowl, mix together the maple syrup, olive oil, and ganjang. In a separate bowl, mix together the oats, almonds, pecans, and pumpkin seeds. Add the liquid mixture to the dry mixture and mix well. Stir in the egg white.

Spread the mixture evenly over a baking sheet and bake for 20 to 25 minutes, tossing the granola every 5 minutes or so, until golden brown. Remove from the oven and let cool for about 15 minutes, then mix in the dried cranberries.

To serve, divide the yogurt between four serving bowls and top each with some granola and one-quarter of the blueberries and peach, then garnish with the mint, if desired.

AMISAN SOOKTI

A few years ago, I was asked by an editor of a Korean food magazine to taste through more than fifty jangs from all parts of Korea. Together with a panel of other chefs and experts, we set up shop in a conference room in Seoul and began to taste. There were ganjangs from all over the peninsula. They ranged from delicate straw-colored liquid ganjangs to heartier, almost meaty, more viscous ones. As you might imagine, when tasting straight jang, no chaser, keeping your palate from burning out is a challenge. After a while, despite my best efforts, the jangs blended together in my mind—until I sipped from a small ramekin of dark brown ganjang. The ganjang's flavor was so strong, it was like a creature bursting forth from the liquid. It was bracingly salty and robust. It burst with *gamchilmat*, "profound flavor." But it wasn't just the taste that struck me. Memories of my childhood flooded unbidden into my mind. *This*, I thought, *is the jang of my father's mother, Yoo Jong-Yeon*. Immediately, I was transported to visits to her hometown in the Boeun region, a few hours from Seoul. When I looked at the bottle, I was amazed that this jang actually came from the same area where she had lived and where my father grew up, a rolling, mountainous land still relatively untouched by Seoul's manic energy. Since my grandmother passed away, we hadn't been back to Boeun often, but I was intrigued by this familiar flavor, tasted

years later in the most unexpected circumstance, and by the artisan who made it: Woo Chun-Hong.

The village of Sookti, high up on a mountainside, is reached via a series of tight switchbacks winding up from the valley floor. The neat fields of cultivated jujubes give way to pine trees and oaks. Sookti is a small town, or rather, village, made up of a dozen or so houses on a steep slope nestled between pine and oak trees. There are no restaurants or businesses, just family houses. In fact, the houses belong to just one family. Of the fifteen or so inhabitants of Sookti, all are members in one way or another of the Woo family.

The town dates back over six hundred years, to when a member of the Joseon royal household, surname Woo, was exiled by the king and took all the Woos from Seoul with him to settle here. It is not where Woo Chun-Hong thought she would end up. Though she was born here, Chun-Hong, a woman with a wide smile and eyes that nearly crinkle shut when she does, spent most of her life in Seoul. For years, she ran a vintage furniture store in Insadong, Seoul's famous antiques street. She and her husband, Mike, raised their children there, venturing back to the village only to visit her mother, Lee Pong-Sun, for holidays, much like my own father did his mother. But nine years ago, after their children had moved out, they moved back permanently.

Mike jokes that he married Chun-Hong for her village, but it is only half a joke. He took to village life immediately. He built himself a workshop where he makes toy riding horses and enthusiastically joined the communal lunches and dinners eaten in a small pavilion during the winter. Chun-Hong, on the other hand, didn't know what to do with herself, back in this tiny town of her youth. Mike suggested she turn her mother's hobby into a business. A portion of the back patio of Pong-Sun's house, like all those in Sookti, is given over to jangdok. Pong-Sun had become famous for her ganjang, which is not too difficult in a village of only fifteen, and her daughter, with free time on her hands, saw an opportunity. At first, Chun-Hong followed her mother's traditional recipes, making small batches of doenjang and ganjang that she and Mike sold to a friend of his, who ran a large company, to give as holiday gifts.

For a time, it seemed to be working. But Chun-Hong felt angry. She was angry at Mike for bringing her back to Sookti; impatient with her mother, who moved slowly and clung stubbornly to tradition; and frustrated with herself for being stuck. To make matters worse, after a few years, jang sales bottomed out, leaving Chun-Hong with seventy jangdok, purchased from an artisan in Ulsan, full of jang but with no buyers. Chun-Hong yearned to return to Seoul, away from this sleepy village on the side of a mountain. Instead, she began to visit Beopjusa, a nearly 1,500-year-old Buddhist temple near Sookti. Meeting with the monks there, she deepened her study of Buddhism, with its underlying philosophy of acceptance. Her life, at that very moment, with all its anger, impatience, and frustration, was complete just as it was. As the monks taught her, along with those feelings of suffering was the possibility of accepting each and every moment.

They were, in fact, gates through which she could reach enlightenment. Chun-Hong listened closely to the teachings, and slowly, her joy began to return. Walking and working among the jangdok one morning, she finally realized she belonged just where she was, doing exactly what she was doing.

She began to fully inhabit jang making, suffusing her intentions and ideas along with her labor into the process. Instead of simply re-creating her mother's recipes, she brought herself to the recipes. For instance, she experimented with adding thirty-year-old Pu-erh tea to the jangdok along with the meju instead of the traditional water. She allowed her meju to age in the open elements, letting the mountain biome penetrate the blocks of soybean. She made jang with joy and pure intention. Even to this day, Chun-Hong recites 108 vows of repentance to clarify her intention every morning before working with jang.

Chun-Hong's jang—marketed under the name Amisan Sookti—has become renowned for its rustic yet refined flavor, the flavor that drew me to it all the way from Seoul. In 2019, it won the Best Fermented Product award given by the Slow Food Cultural Center. And though the demand has grown, Chun-Hong's operation remains small. She wants to touch every element of her jang. So it is that she produces only 80 gallons (300 L) of ganjang a year.

These days, Chun-Hong seems truly happy in Sookti. On any given day, you'll find her and her mother making the day's dubu in a large outdoor gamasot, stirring the milky liquid with a large paddle while Mike feeds the fire with wood scraps from his workshop. It is the same wood-fired pot in which she boils down the soybeans in January when they come from local farmers in the valley. The family gathers for lunch around a long table at Chun-Hong's home. The table is laden with fermented biji (soybean pulp left over from making dubu), fresh dubu with seasoned ganjang, fresh kimchi, blanched butterbur with doenjang, and bonnet bellflower roots. After lunch, Chun-Hong tends to her neat rows of jangdok just next door. Each vessel is covered with rice paper, secured with string, and then sealed with a terra-cotta top. Like all artisanal jang making, her work depends on the season. In spring, she separates the doenjang from the ganjang. Usually this process is hastened along by the help of her six brothers and sisters. Unlike more commercial artisans, Chun-Hong relies entirely on her own senses rather than precise measuring tools. She breaks the meju by hand, feeling for the hardened clumps of black mold that need removing. With a small wooden spoon, she tastes the strong, meaty liquid of the ganjang and the even richer flecks of doenjang. Chun-Hong sifts the remaining liquid from the jangdok, transferring it to another container. This will be boiled and aged for another two years, at least. The solids, of course, will be repotted and aged to become doenjang. It's hard work, and hot, too.

Chun-Hong and Mike share one small studio, which serves as a showroom for the rare souls who make it to Sookti as well as a teahouse for Chun-Hong's beloved Pu-erh teas and a gallery of a local artist's work. His paintings—neat, almost abstract grids—reveal themselves upon closer inspection to be brushstroke figures prostrating themselves, over and over again. It is an act of devotion, not too dissimilar from Chun-Hong's daily practice with jang. She is a woman who fully inhabits her life, her place, her time, her home. And it is a journey, she says, that began with jang and expands over time, but lives right in the moment.

DOENJANG

GREEN BEANS *with* SESAME VINAIGRETTE
참깨 비네그렛을 곁들인 그린빈

Kosher salt

7 ounces (200 g) green beans

1½ tablespoons sesame seeds, finely ground, plus a pinch of whole seeds for garnish

1 tablespoon brown rice vinegar

1½ teaspoons hansik doenjang

1 tablespoon toasted sesame oil

2 teaspoons extra-virgin olive oil

1 teaspoon hansik ganjang

2¼ teaspoons honey

1½ teaspoons crushed almonds

A fine line separates banchan from a standard appetizer. One way to think of it is that banchan relies on the other aspects of the meal to be best enjoyed, whereas an appetizer is self-contained. This green bean recipe lives just on the appetizer side of the street, and it's the vinaigrette dressing—which combines the gamchilmat of doenjang with the acidity of vinegar and the nuttiness of sesame seeds—that gives it the balance to stand on its own. Despite its fulsome flavor, the dish is completely vegan; it pairs excellently with light, toasty white wines like a sauvignon blanc or an aligoté.

NOTE: Bread, cheese, and dubu go well with these green beans.

Bring 8⅓ cups (2 L) well-salted water to a boil. Fill a bowl with equal parts ice and water. Blanch the green beans in the boiling water for 1½ to 2 minutes, then transfer them to the ice bath to stop the cooking. Once cool, drain the green beans and trim the ends.

In a large bowl, whisk together the ground sesame seeds, vinegar, doenjang, sesame oil, olive oil, ganjang, and honey.

To serve, add the green beans to the dressing and toss to coat, then top with the almonds and whole sesame seeds.

ROOT VEGETABLE SALAD

뿌리채소 샐러드

SERVES 4

1½ cups (200 g) sliced peeled fingerling or other small potatoes (sliced ½ inch/1 cm thick)

⅓ butternut squash, peeled, seeded, and cut into 1-inch-thick (2.5 cm) rounds

1 sweet potato, peeled and cut into ½-inch-thick (1 cm) slices

8 large baby carrots, halved

½ golden beet, peeled and cut into ½-inch-thick (1 cm) slices

2 tablespoons extra-virgin olive oil

1 tablespoon fresh thyme leaves

Kosher salt

½ red beet, peeled and cut into ½-inch-thick (1 cm) slices

⅓ cup (90 g) BBQ doenjang (see page 54)

¼ cup (20 g) sliced almonds

4 or 5 carrot greens, roughly torn

Freshly ground black pepper

This simple autumn or winter salad relies on the stored sugars in the root vegetables, brought out during their roasting, and the nutty gamchilmat of BBQ doenjang, brought out during its reduction. It's a hearty salad, filling enough to be a vegan main course, if you like. Though it's super easy to make, there are two moments to be watchful of. The first is aesthetic. When tossing the vegetables, keep the red beets separate, unless you don't mind all the vegetables taking on a scarlet hue. The second is that due to their varied density, each of the vegetables cooks at a slightly different rate. Generally the denser the vegetable, the longer the cooking time. While roasting, periodically stick a fork in them to see which are tender (and thus ready to come out of the oven) and which need more time.

Preheat the oven to 425°F (220°C). Line a baking sheet with parchment paper.

In a large bowl, toss together the potatoes, squash, sweet potato, carrots, and golden beet with half the olive oil, half the thyme, and a pinch of salt. In a separate bowl, toss together the red beet with the remaining olive oil and thyme and another pinch of salt.

Spread the vegetables out on the prepared baking sheet and roast for 15 minutes, checking occasionally to make sure the thinly sliced vegetables don't burn.

Meanwhile, in a small bowl, mix together the BBQ doenjang with 3 tablespoons (45 ml) water.

After 15 minutes, remove the vegetables from the oven (leave the oven on) and toss in a bowl with the thinned BBQ doenjang. Mix well, then place the vegetables back on the pan and roast for 5 minutes more. Serve immediately, topped with the sliced almonds, carrot greens, and pepper to taste.

GREEK BARLEY SALAD *with* DOENJANG VINAIGRETTE

그리스식 보리 샐러드와 된장 비네그렛 드레싱

SERVES 2

¾ cup (120 g) uncooked barley

1 head baby romaine lettuce

FOR THE DOENJANG VINAIGRETTE

1½ tablespoons white wine vinegar

1 tablespoon hansik doenjang

1½ teaspoons honey

½ teaspoon Dijon mustard

1 tablespoon plus 2¼ teaspoons extra-virgin olive oil

¼ cup (2 g) fresh parsley, coarsely chopped

¼ cup (2 g) fresh mint, coarsely chopped

1 medium tomato, diced

⅓ medium cucumber, diced

2 ounces (60 g) feta cheese, cut into ⅓-inch (1 cm) cubes

8 green olives, pitted and sliced

10 black olives, pitted and sliced

1 small radish, cut into sixths

At the heart of this summertime recipe is gangdoenjang, a thickened doenjang often served over rice and with lettuce wraps. It is earthy, filling comfort food, perfect in the warm weather when vegetables are at their freshest. This salad combines the gravitas of the thickened doenjang, barley (which, according to Korean dietary lore, has refreshing energy), and the easily recognizable flavors of a Greek salad. Instead of cooking the gangdoenjang to concentrate it as you do for Gangdoenjang Bibimbap (page 129), you'll thicken it with the classic vinaigrette ingredients. The Mediterranean mixture of feta, olives, cucumber, and tomato forms the high notes, while the doenjang and barley ground the salad in the soil.

Rinse the barley well and place in a medium pot with 3⅓ cups (800 ml) water. Bring to a boil over medium heat, then cook for 20 minutes. Remove from the heat, rinse the barley in cold water, and set aside.

Separate the leaves, one by one, from the head of lettuce. Wash under cold water then allow to dry (or spin-dry).

MAKE THE VINAIGRETTE: In a small bowl, mix together the vinegar, doenjang, honey, and mustard. Pass the mixture through a sieve to remove any larger chunks of doenjang. While whisking continuously, add the olive oil in a slow, steady stream and whisk to emulsify.

To serve, mix the barley with half the dressing and place in the center of a serving platter. Pour the remaining dressing over (use as much as you like) and sprinkle with the parsley and mint. Ring the barley with the tomato, cucumber, feta, olives, and radish. Serve with the lettuce leaves.

DOENJANG HUMMUS

된장 후무스

SERVES 2

½ cup (100 g) dried chickpeas or 8 ounces (230 g) canned chickpeas

1 tablespoon sesame seeds, finely ground

1½ tablespoons blended doenjang (see page 53)

1½ teaspoons honey

Juice of ½ lemon

2 tablespoons extra-virgin olive oil

Pinch of freshly ground black pepper

Pinch of doenjang powder (see page 48)

Pinch of gochujang powder (see page 48)

1 cup (80 g) mini carrots, rinsed

½ cup (80 g) cherry tomatoes, halved

2 celery stalks, cut into 3-inch (7.5 cm) pieces

Crackers or chips

Hummus is like the distant cousin of doenjang. Both are made from beans, both are vegan, both are astonishingly versatile. This recipe is the perfect accompaniment with crudités or chips for a mineral-forward chardonnay like one from Santa Barbara or a Chinon cab franc from the Loire Valley. You can also change the recipe seasonally. In the summer, I use fava beans. In the springtime, green peas. Sometimes I'll stick closer to home, using the yellow soybean that we use for the doenjang itself. The magic is in how the fermented bean interacts with the fresh ones, no matter which bean you use.

If using dried chickpeas, fully submerge the chickpeas in water and let soak overnight. Drain, then transfer to a large pot with 4¼ cups (1 L) water and bring to a boil over medium heat. Reduce the heat to low and simmer for 40 minutes, until the chickpeas are cooked through (they should be soft but not mushy), then remove from the heat. Reserve ⅔ cup (150 ml) of the cooking water, then drain. (If using canned chickpeas, skip the soaking and boiling step, but reserve ½ cup/120 ml of the liquid from the can.)

In a blender, mix together half the reserved chickpea water, the chickpeas, sesame seeds, doenjang, honey, and lemon juice. With the blender running, gradually add the remaining chickpea water and 1½ tablespoons of the olive oil and blend until the texture is creamy.

To serve, spread the hummus on a plate, making a small well in the center. Sprinkle it with the remaining ½ tablespoon olive oil, the pepper, doenjang powder, and gochujang powder. Serve with the carrots, tomatoes, celery, and crackers alongside.

BAECHU SOGOGI DOENJANG JEONGOL

배추 쇠고기 된장전골

Cabbage Beef Doenjang Stew

SERVES 3 OR 4

FOR THE BEEF BRISKET AND BROTH

7 ounces (200 g) beef brisket, trimmed

¼ medium daikon radish, peeled and quartered

¼ onion, coarsely chopped

3 green onions

5 garlic cloves, peeled

FOR THE CABBAGE

½ small napa cabbage, leaves separated

1 tablespoon plus 1 teaspoon hansik ganjang

1½ teaspoons hansik doenjang

1 tablespoon coarsely ground gochugaru

FOR THE SOUP

1½ teaspoons hansik doenjang

2 cups (480 ml) anchovy stock (see page 50)

5 ounces (150 g) dubu, cut into 1½-inch-thick (3.5 cm) squares

¼ cup (75 g) thinly sliced peeled daikon radish (1 by 2 by ⅛-inch/2.5 cm by 5 cm by 3 mm pieces)

¼ zucchini, sliced into ¼-inch-thick (6 mm) half-moons

Historically, since beef was so scarce, Koreans learned to stretch it any way we could. When incorporating beef in a soup, every bit of nourishment from the meat is extracted, which explains why hansik has a long and well-developed culture of beef soup. This soup encapsulates not just Korean cuisine but Korean culture in general. It takes something that is common and plentiful (cabbage) and something that is precious and rare (beef), combining the two to provide not just sustenance but comfort, too. The cabbage imparts its sweetness to the broth while absorbing the flavors of the meat and vegetables with which it is cooked. The combination of anchovy stock and beef stock makes the soup lighter than expected yet dense with gamchilmat.

Before she passed away, I used to make this soup for my mother-in-law when she was sick. She grew up eating doenjang soup but said it was never as good as this. The secret is a high-quality doenjang, which gives the soup its body and irresistible, deeply satisfying flavor.

MAKE THE BRISKET AND BROTH: In a large pot, combine the brisket, daikon, onion, green onions, and garlic. Add 8⅓ cups (2 L) water and bring to a boil over high heat. Reduce the heat to low and cover. Simmer for 1½ to 2 hours, occasionally skimming the top to remove the foam, until the meat is fully cooked: Poke it with a chopstick, and if no blood emerges it is done. Remove the brisket and set aside to cool slightly, then thinly slice. Strain the broth into a container and set aside at room temperature (discard the solids).

MAKE THE CABBAGE: Bring a medium pot of water to a boil. Fill a large bowl with equal parts ice and cold water. Trim the bottom of the cabbage leaves and cut the leaves into quarters. Blanch the cabbage in the boiling water for 1 to 2 minutes, until the leaves are tender, then plunge them into the ice bath to stop cooking. Pat dry and let cool on a baking sheet.

In a small bowl, combine the ganjang, doenjang, and gochugaru and mix well. Massage the seasoning into the cooled cabbage leaves and set aside.

ingredients continue

recipe continues

2 green onions, white parts only, thinly sliced

⅓ red chile, thinly sliced

½ green Cheongyang chile or jalapeño, thinly sliced

1½ teaspoons Korean fish sauce (aekjeot)

3 cups (600 g) cooked rice, for serving

MAKE THE SOUP: Pass the doenjang through a sieve into a large container to make sure there are no larger bean chunks. Add the anchovy stock and 3 cups (720 ml) of the beef brisket broth and stir to combine.

Lay the cabbage leaves at the bottom of a large, wide pot, place the sliced meat in the center, and arrange the dubu, daikon, and zucchini around the meat. Add the stock mixture to the pot and bring to a boil over high heat. Reduce the heat to low and cook for 15 minutes, then add the green onions, red chile, and green chile and season with the fish sauce. Cook for a final 30 seconds, then serve immediately with rice.

DOENJANG JJAJANGMYEON 된장 짜장면
Doenjang Black Noodles

SERVES 2

FOR THE ONION DOENJANG

½ cup (120 ml) neutral oil, such as grapeseed or canola

3 medium onions, cut into ½-inch (1 cm) dice

⅔ cup (200 g) yangjo doenjang

FOR THE JJAJANG MIXTURE

6½ ounces (180 g) pork shoulder, cut into ⅔-inch (1.5 cm) dice

Freshly ground black pepper

½ cabbage, cut into ½-inch (1 cm) dice

1½ zucchini, cut into ½-inch (1 cm) dice

2 teaspoons cornstarch

FOR THE TOPPING AND NOODLES

Kosher salt

2 tablespoons neutral oil, such as grapeseed or canola

2 eggs

14 ounces (400 g) dried kalguksu noodles or dried inaniwa udon (see headnote)

The story of jjajangmyeon begins in Eastern China, where the dish originated as zhájiàngmiàn. A fermented black bean sauce is fried and tossed with noodles. In the late nineteenth century, the dish that would become jjajangmyeon arrived in Korea along with Chinese soldiers who were stationed in Incheon. As with many things—Korean fried chicken, for instance—Koreans made the dish all their own by adding starch and caramel to make noodles served with an even darker and thicker sauce. Today, jjajangmyeon is often inky black. (The key to the color is frying; the key to the thickness is cornstarch.)

Since the 1950s, jjajangmyeon has been ubiquitous in Korea. In every city, big or small, you can get jjajangmyeon twenty-four hours a day from Chinese Korean restaurants. Unlike those deeply satisfying yet cheap versions, this one forgoes the added colors and chemicals that have become part of the jjajang sauce and instead uses doenjang. The result is healthier and a little lighter in hue. As for the noodles, traditionally jjajang noodles are made with carbonated water and wheat flour and are extremely elastic. But those noodles are hard to come by, even in Korea. Kalguksu, similarly made with wheat flour, are just as delicious and much easier to find. Udon and tagliarini work well, too.

MAKE THE ONION DOENJANG: Heat a deep, heavy-bottomed pan over medium heat. Add the oil and reduce the heat to low. When the oil is shimmering, add the onions and cook, stirring occasionally, until soft and translucent, about 20 minutes. Add the doenjang and stir-fry for 5 minutes, until the doenjang turns a light brown.

MAKE THE JJAJANG MIXTURE: Pat the pork dry and season with pepper to taste. Add the pork to the pan with the onion doenjang and cook, stirring frequently, until evenly cooked, about 1 minute. Increase the heat to high and add the cabbage and zucchini. Stir well, then sauté for 5 minutes more. If the vegetables begin to stick to the bottom of the pan, add a tablespoon or two of water, stirring and scraping up the solids so they don't burn.

Meanwhile, in a small bowl, stir together the cornstarch and ⅓ cup plus 1 tablespoon (100 ml) water to make a slurry. When the jjajang mixture starts to bubble, add the slurry to the pan and

reduce the heat to medium. Simmer for 1 to 2 minutes, until the mixture thickens, then remove from the heat.

MAKE THE TOPPING AND NOODLES: Bring 4 quarts (4 L) well-salted water to a boil in a large pot over high heat.

Meanwhile, in a small skillet, heat the oil over high heat until shimmering. Add one egg, keeping the yolk whole. While holding the pan on an angle, baste the egg with the oil until the white is opaque and the yolk, though slightly covered, is runny, about 1 minute. Transfer to a paper towel–lined plate to drain and repeat with the second egg.

Add the noodles to the boiling water and cook according to the package directions (usually 7 to 8 minutes), agitating the noodles as they cook so they do not stick. Drain the noodles and empty the pot. Run the noodles under cold water to remove the starch from their surface and return them to the pot. Add the jjajang mixture to the noodles and stir together. Cook over high heat for a minute or two to warm through.

To serve, divide the noodles evenly between two bowls and top each with an egg.

HONGHAP DOENJANG GUK 홍합 된장국
Mussel Doenjang Soup

SERVES 2

7 ounces (200 g) mussels

2 cups (480 ml) anchovy stock (see page 50; see Note)

1 tablespoon blended doenjang (see page 53)

2 garlic cloves, thinly sliced

1 green onion, white part only, finely chopped

4 cups packed (150 g) fresh spinach, leaves stemmed

½ small Cheongyang chile or jalapeño, thinly sliced

½ small red chile, thinly sliced

2 cups (400 g) cooked rice or a loaf of crusty French bread, for serving

The best spinach in Korea comes from the city of Pohang on the eastern coast of the peninsula, where the plants, buffeted by the ocean wind, huddle close to the earth and develop thick, strong, and sweet leaves. But even if you can't get that specific type of spinach, called pohangcho, this spinachy doenjang seafood soup is still a winner. It's a flavor combination familiar to any lover of a classic Provençal mussel stew. The doenjang plays the part of tomato, deepening the broth, while the chiles add pops of heat. In Korea, we eat this during the winter—prime season for mussels and spinach—but it's not so heavy that it shouldn't be eaten year-round.

NOTE: You can use water instead of anchovy stock, but if you do, add an extra 2 teaspoons blended doenjang.

Rinse the mussels well, discarding any open ones. Remove their beards by tugging on the small, tough ligament protruding from the shell.

Pour the stock into a small stockpot, add the doenjang, and stir well to combine. Add the mussels and garlic and bring to a boil over high heat. Cook until the mussel shells open, about 10 minutes, then reduce the heat to low. Add the green onion and cook for 5 minutes more to impart a deeper flavor to the liquid, occasionally skimming the top to remove any foam or floating debris. Remove the mussels from the broth and set aside (discard any that don't open).

Add the spinach and sliced chiles to the broth, increase the heat to high, and boil for a minute or two, until the spinach leaves have lost all their toughness. Remove from the heat, return the mussels to the pot, and serve immediately with rice.

GANGDOENJANG BIBIMBAP

강된장 비빔밥

SERVES 2

FOR THE GANGDOENJANG

1 cup (240 ml) anchovy stock (see page 50)

2½ tablespoons blended doenjang (see page 53)

1½ teaspoons gochujang

1½ teaspoons cornstarch

1 tablespoon plus 1 teaspoon neutral oil, such as grapeseed or canola

3½ ounces (100 g) beef shoulder, thinly sliced

½ cup (50 g) diced peeled daikon radish

¼ onion, diced

⅓ zucchini, diced

3 pyogo (shiitake) mushrooms, stemmed and diced

1 red chile, thinly sliced

1 green Cheongyang chile or jalapeño, thinly sliced

⅓ green onion, white part only, finely diced

1 garlic clove, finely diced

TO SERVE

2 cups (400 g) cooked rice

2 lettuce leaves, cut into 2-inch (5 cm) squares

12 perilla leaves, cut into 2-inch (5 cm) squares

1 red radish, thinly sliced

½ teaspoon toasted sesame oil, for garnish

Pinch of sesame seeds, for garnish

Bibimbap usually involves mixing vegetables with rice, but in this case, the sauce itself is the main ingredient. *Gang* means "thickened" or "fortified," and here the doenjang is sufficiently thickened to become the star of the show. Since you can store the sauce for up to a week, this is a perfect weeknight dinner when you're short on time. (For other uses of gangdoenjang, see the Greek Barley Salad with Doenjang Vinaigrette, page 116).

MAKE THE GANGDOENJANG: In a small bowl, mix the stock, doenjang, and gochujang well and set aside.

In another small bowl, stir together the cornstarch and 1 tablespoon plus 1 teaspoon water to create a slurry. Set aside.

Heat a large pot over medium heat. Add the neutral oil. When it is shimmering, add the beef and stir-fry for about 1 minute. Add the daikon and onion and cook, stirring continuously, for 2 minutes more, until both soften. Add the zucchini and mushrooms and cook for 2 minutes. Add the stock mixture little by little, stirring and scraping up the vegetables and meat stuck to the bottom of the pot as you go (these are the most delicious parts). Add the red chile, green chile, green onion, and garlic and cook for 1 minute more. Add a tablespoon or two of water if too much liquid boils down during this process. Stir in the cornstarch slurry, bring the mixture to a boil, and remove from the heat.

Serve immediately with the rice, lettuce and perilla leaves, and sliced radish. Garnish with the sesame oil and sesame seeds.

SSAMJANG CACIO E PEPE

쌈장 카치오 에 페페

SERVES 2 OR 3

1 tablespoon plus
1 teaspoon kosher salt

6 ounces (180 g) dried
pasta, such as casarecce
or penne

Extra-virgin olive oil

2¼ cups (530 ml) chicken
stock (see page 50, or use
store-bought)

⅔ cup (150 ml) heavy
cream

2 tablespoons ssamjang
(see page 53)

3 ounces (40 g) pecorino
cheese, grated

1 tablespoon plus
1 teaspoon unsalted
butter, cut into cubes

Freshly ground black
pepper

This recipe takes the well-known flavor profile of cacio e pepe, the Italian black pepper and cheese pasta, and adds to it ssamjang, a jang mother sauce combining gochujang and doenjang. Comparing the rich, creamy pasta dish without ssamjang and with ssamjang immediately brings into clarity the character of the sauce, which cuts through the signature richness of cacio e pepe.

Fill a large pot with 2 quarts (2 L) water and add the salt. Bring to a boil over high heat. Add the pasta and cook for 3 minutes less than the package instructs for al dente. Drain the pasta, toss it with olive oil, and let cool.

In a large flat-bottomed pan, combine the stock, cream, and ssamjang and bring to a boil over medium-high heat. Reduce the heat to low, fold in the cooked pasta, and cook, stirring continuously, until the sauce has thickened, 7 to 8 minutes.

Add the pecorino and butter and cook, stirring, until both have melted. Serve immediately, topped with a few generous turns of pepper.

STEAMED COD *with* DOENJANG BÉARNAISE

생선찜과 된장 베어네이즈 소스

SERVES 2

5 ounces (150 g) fingerling potatoes, peeled

2½ teaspoons kosher salt

½ cup (120 ml) anchovy stock (see page 50)

¼ cup (60 ml) white wine vinegar

1 garlic clove, coarsely chopped

2 egg yolks

7 tablespoons (100 g) unsalted butter, cut into cubes, at room temperature

2 tablespoons blended doenjang (see page 53)

2¼ teaspoons toasted sesame oil

1 tablespoon finely chopped fresh parsley

2 (10½-ounce/300 g) black cod fillets, 1 to 1½ inches (2.5 to 4 cm) thick

½ teaspoon coarse salt

1 tablespoon fresh chervil leaves

Like Ssamjang Cacio e Pepe (page 130), this recipe highlights the power of jang. It's also an example of how jang and dairy—butter, specifically—are perfect complements for each other. Béarnaise sauce, the offspring of a hollandaise, can sometimes be so rich and heavy it is all you can taste. Lightening the sauce with fish stock and cutting the butter's richness with the gamchilmat of doenjang lets the sweetness of the steamed fish shine through. If you don't have black cod, any fatty white fish such as sea bass or halibut works well.

Fill a large stockpot with water, add the potatoes and the kosher salt, and bring to a boil over high heat. Reduce the heat to low and cook until the potatoes are fork-tender, about 15 minutes. Drain the potatoes and let them cool to room temperature.

Meanwhile, in a small pot, combine the stock, vinegar, and garlic and cook over high heat until reduced by half, about 5 minutes. Remove from the heat. Carefully strain the vinegar mixture into a heatproof bowl (discard the garlic) and let cool.

Bring a medium pot of water to a boil over high heat, then reduce the heat to maintain a simmer. Add the egg yolks to the bowl with the vinegar mixture and set the bowl over the pot, being careful not to let the bottom of the bowl touch the water. While whisking rapidly, begin to add the butter, a little bit at a time, until all the butter has been incorporated (the vinegar should be warm but not too hot, or the butter will separate). Add the doenjang and sesame oil and whisk until the mixture emulsifies. Strain the doenjang béarnaise, if you like, then add half the parsley. Keep warm.

Season the fish fillets with the coarse salt. Fill the bottom of a stacking steamer with water and bring to a boil. Set the fillets on the upper level of the steamer and steam for 12 to 15 minutes, depending on thickness, until warm and opaque. Remove and let rest for 3 minutes. While the fish rests, reheat the fingerling potatoes in the steamer for 3 minutes.

To serve, divide the doenjang béarnaise between two plates, then top with the potatoes and steamed fish. Finish with the remaining parsley and the chervil and serve immediately.

DOVER SOLE *with* DOENJANG CAPER SAUCE

된장 케이퍼 소스를 곁들인 서대구이

SERVES 2

FOR THE DOENJANG CAPER SAUCE

2 tablespoons neutral oil, such as grapeseed or canola

2 tablespoons toasted sesame oil

6 garlic cloves, coarsely chopped

1 tablespoon capers, finely chopped

1 tablespoon hansik doenjang

FOR THE DOVER SOLE

2 skin-on Dover sole fillets (11 ounces/300 g)

½ teaspoon kosher salt

½ teaspoon freshly ground white pepper

2 tablespoons all-purpose flour

2 lemons, halved

1 tablespoon plus 1 teaspoon neutral oil, such as grapeseed or canola

2 cups (100 g) spinach

1 teaspoon finely chopped fresh parsley

Cooking fish à la meunière—that is, dredging it in flour and panfrying, often in butter, until it is golden, crispy, comforting, transcendent, and delicious—is clearly not a Korean technique. (We are a rice-based, not wheat-based, and largely nondairy culture.) Nor is there any Dover sole in Seoul. Yet this recipe demonstrates how widely and fruitfully jang can be used and how well it plays with Western flavors. Doenjang transforms the classic French sauce. It replaces the anchovies traditionally used, while the sesame oil gives the nuttiness you would normally get from the browned butter. The sauce works just as well on scallops or on, really, any flaky white-fleshed fish like halibut, flounder, cod, and hake. It is a vegan sauce, which you could also serve on cauliflower and asparagus or turnips and Broccolini. (It works better for root vegetables than leafy ones.)

MAKE THE SAUCE: In a medium saucepan, combine the neutral oil and sesame oil and heat over medium heat until shimmering. Add the garlic and cook until lightly golden, about 3 minutes, being careful not to let it brown. Add the capers and doenjang. Mix well and remove from the heat. Set aside.

MAKE THE SOLE: Season the fish fillets with the salt and white pepper. Sprinkle evenly with the flour. Heat a large cast-iron pan over medium heat. Place the lemon halves in the pan, cut side down, and char until well browned, about 1 minute. Remove and set aside.

Add the neutral oil to the skillet and warm until shimmering. Add the sole, skin side down, and cook, without moving it, for 4 to 5 minutes. When the edges of the fillets turn opaque, flip the fish and add the doenjang caper sauce to the pan. Cook, basting the fish with the sauce, for 1 to 2 minutes more. Remove the fish and set aside. (The fish will be 80 to 90 percent cooked, but will continue to cook while resting.)

Add the spinach to the pan and cook until wilted, about 1 minute. Remove from the heat.

To serve, divide the spinach evenly between two plates, then place a fillet on each. Pour the doenjang caper sauce from the pan over the fish, then sprinkle with the parsley. Finish with a squeeze of juice from the charred lemons.

BBQ-GLAZED CHICKEN *with* DOENJANG RISOTTO

바베큐 치킨과 된장 리조토

SERVES 2

1 cup (185 g) uncooked glutinous rice

2 bone-in, skin-on chicken breasts

3½ tablespoons (60 g) BBQ doenjang (see page 54)

1 tablespoon neutral oil, such as grapeseed or canola

2 garlic cloves, crushed

1 cup (240 ml) chicken stock (see page 50, or use store-bought)

⅓ cup (80 ml) heavy cream

1 tablespoon blended doenjang (see page 53)

⅓ cup (30 g) shaved Parmigiano Reggiano cheese

1½ tablespoons unsalted butter

Freshly ground black pepper

Risotto feels like one of the few natural bridges between Italian and Korean cookery. When I opened Mingles, I kept looking for a solution to making a risotto that felt equally at home in both the Italian and the Korean kitchen. I found the answer in godubap, a method of steaming rice most often used for making makgeolli (rice wine) or cho (vinegar). Traditionally in godubap, you steam normal rice, but for this risotto, you'll use glutinous rice you soak overnight, which allows you to cook the rice ahead and save it while retaining the mouthfeel and texture. (Nothing is worse than a mushy risotto.) Because doenjang plays well with cream and cheese, the result is an unusually deeply flavored risotto, which is comforting on cold days but not so heavy as to necessitate a post-meal nap.

For a complete meal, I pair the risotto with a very simple glazed chicken breast marinated in BBQ doenjang. It's absurdly easy to make and extremely delicious.

Soak the glutinous rice in water to cover overnight. In the morning, drain the rice and spread it out on a piece of wet cheesecloth. Fill the bottom of a stacking steamer with water and bring to a boil. Drape the cheesecloth with the rice inside the upper level of the steamer and steam it for 30 minutes, until the rice is cooked through and translucent. Spread it on a tray and let cool to room temperature.

Meanwhile, toss together the chicken and BBQ doenjang in a container. Cover and marinate in the refrigerator for 30 to 40 minutes.

When ready to cook, in a cast-iron skillet, heat the oil over medium heat until shimmering. Add the garlic and cook for a few minutes, until golden. Add the chicken breasts, skin side down, and reduce the heat to low. Cook, flipping the chicken regularly to keep the doenjang from burning, until well charred on the outside and opaque in the center, 12 to 15 minutes. Remove it from the pan and let rest.

While the chicken is resting, add the stock, cream, 1½ cups (280 g) of the cooked glutinous rice, and the blended doenjang to the now empty pan and bring to a boil over medium heat. Cook, stirring

constantly so the rice does not stick to the bottom of the pan, for 5 to 7 minutes, until the rice has fully absorbed the cream. Remove the pan from the heat, add the cheese and butter, and mix until both are fully incorporated. Finish with a few turns of pepper.

To serve, divide the risotto evenly between two plates. Slice the chicken into bite-size pieces and serve atop the risotto.

SAMGYEOPSAL SUYUK-GWA MUSAENGCHAE

삼겹살 수육과 무생채

Boiled Pork Belly with Quick Daikon Kimchi

SERVES 2 OR 3

FOR THE PORK BELLY

10½ ounces (300 g) skin-on pork belly

⅓ cup (100 g) yangjo doenjang

9 or 10 green onions, cut into large pieces

⅓ onion, cut into large pieces

6 garlic cloves, peeled

10 whole black peppercorns

1 bay leaf

FOR THE BRINED CABBAGE

1 tablespoon kosher salt

12 napa cabbage leaves (inner leaves only)

FOR THE QUICK DAIKON KIMCHI

1 cup (100 g) thinly sliced peeled daikon radish

¼ teaspoon salt

1 teaspoon sugar

1 teaspoon brown rice vinegar

1 teaspoon toasted sesame oil

½ teaspoon hansik ganjang

½ teaspoon coarsely ground gochugaru

½ teaspoon sesame seeds, coarsely ground

ingredients continue

Traditionally, once a year in late autumn or early winter, Koreans come together for kimjang, the process of making kimchi. It's a labor-intensive and joyous period, similar in some ways to the grape harvest in Italy or France. Kimjang is important, not just because it furnishes our family with a year's worth of kimchi but also because it reinforces the ties of friendship in our community. Even though the kimchi will ferment over the year until next year's kimjang, we use some of it that very day for a celebratory dinner of suyuk. *Su* means "water" and *yuk* means "meat," so technically, any meat could be suyuk. But pork belly, with its layers of fat that soften and render so beautifully in the braise, is so common that suyuk has become synonymous with braised pork belly. And it just happens to pair perfectly with the as-yet-unfermented kimchi called musaengchae. The intense fattiness of the pork belly is cut through by the tartness of the musaengchae. A dab of sweet-and-salty ssamjang lends the final touch.

MAKE THE PORK BELLY: Rinse the pork belly well in cold water, then blot dry with a paper towel.

In a medium pot, whisk the doenjang into 4¼ cups (1 L) water. Add the green onions, onion, garlic, peppercorns, bay leaf, and pork belly and bring to a boil over high heat. Allow to boil for 10 to 15 minutes, then cover the pot, reduce the heat to low, and simmer for 1 hour, until the meat is fully cooked: Poke it with a chopstick, and if no blood emerges it is done.

MEANWHILE, BRINE THE CABBAGE: In a large bowl, combine 2 cups (480 ml) water and the salt. Submerge the cabbage leaves in the brine and soak for 30 minutes, then rinse under running water to remove the salt. Drain the cabbage, squeezing it tightly to remove any extra water.

MAKE THE QUICK DAIKON KIMCHI: In a small bowl, gently toss together the daikon and salt. Let sit for 30 minutes, then rinse under running water to remove the salt. Drain the daikon, squeezing it tightly to remove any extra water.

recipe continues

1 teaspoon saeujeot
(salted shrimp; optional)

2 garlic cloves, sliced

1 tablespoon ssamjang
(see page 53)

1 teaspoon toasted
sesame oil

In a medium bowl, mix together the sugar, vinegar, sesame oil, ganjang, gochugaru, and sesame seeds. Gently add the daikon and toss to coat.

When the pork belly is cooked, remove it from the liquid and let rest until cool enough to handle, about 10 minutes, then slice into ⅓-inch-thick (0.75 cm) pieces.

Serve the pork belly, daikon kimchi, and brined cabbage on a platter, accompanied by the saeujeot, if desired, and sliced garlic. Top with the ssamjang and sesame oil.

DOENJANG BBQ LAMB *with* COUSCOUS
된장 양갈비 바베큐

SERVES 2

**FOR THE LAMB AND
VEGETABLES**

18 ounces (500 g) lamb
rib, cut into double-rib
segments if cooking in
the oven or single-rib
segments if using a grill

⅓ cup (90 g) BBQ
doenjang (see page 54)

2 tablespoons neutral
oil, such as grapeseed
or canola

1 garlic clove, crushed

2 thyme sprigs

⅓ head broccoli, cut into
bite-size pieces

4 button mushrooms,
cleaned and stemmed

1 small sweet potato,
scrubbed and halved
lengthwise

2 tablespoons extra-virgin
olive oil

Pinch of kosher salt

Pinch of freshly ground
black pepper

**FOR THE COUSCOUS
SALAD**

½ cup (120 ml) chicken
stock (see page 50, or use
store-bought)

½ cup (120 ml) vegetable
stock

1 cup (150 g) uncooked
couscous

2 teaspoons hansik
ganjang

ingredients continue

Neither lamb nor mutton is used in hansik. In fact, the first time I
had lamb was when I was working as a cook at Vincent's, an Italian
restaurant in Seoul. I was immediately hooked. For the most part,
Koreans don't prefer gamy meat (it's why we often take the extra
step of blanching our meats before braising them). But when lamb is
marinated with doenjang, that fatty gaminess is transformed into a
perfectly balanced, deeply flavored meat. Add to that the sweetness
of the flame (thanks to the Maillard reaction), and barbecued lamb
rivals the hallowed samgyeopsal and famed galbi.

MAKE THE LAMB AND VEGETABLES: In a large container, rub
the lamb with the doenjang. Add the neutral oil, garlic, and thyme,
cover, and let rest in the refrigerator for at least 2 hours and up to
overnight, or at room temperature for 2 hours.

Meanwhile, in another large bowl, toss the broccoli, mushrooms,
and sweet potato with the olive oil, salt, and pepper and set aside.

If necessary, allow the meat to come to room temperature for
30 minutes to 1 hour before cooking. Meanwhile, preheat a grill
to high.

recipe continues

2 teaspoons extra-virgin
olive oil

Zest of ½ lemon

¼ cup (3 g) fresh parsley,
chopped

Place the lamb and sweet potatoes on the grill. Cook for 15 to
20 minutes, turning the lamb and the potatoes frequently to keep
the doenjang from burning, until all sides of the lamb are cooked
evenly and the internal temperature reaches 140° to 145°F (60° to
63°C). Remove the lamb and sweet potatoes from the heat and set
aside to rest. Place the mushrooms and broccoli at the outside edges
of the grill and let cook for 5 minutes, until lightly charred.

MEANWHILE, MAKE THE COUSCOUS SALAD: In a pot, combine
the chicken and vegetable stocks and bring to a boil over high heat.
Place the couscous in a large bowl. Pour the boiling stock over the
couscous, cover, and let sit for 10 minutes. Uncover and stir in the
ganjang, olive oil, and lemon zest. Sprinkle with the parsley.

To serve, plate the individual lamb chops with the grilled
vegetables and serve the couscous salad in a bowl alongside.

ALMOND DOENJANG CROISSANT

아몬드 된장 크루아상

SERVES 4

FOR THE ALMOND CREAM

1 egg

¼ teaspoon kosher salt

1½ tablespoons dark rum (optional)

5 tablespoons (80 g) unsalted butter, cut into cubes, at room temperature

1 tablespoon yangjo doenjang

1 cup (80 g) almond flour

⅔ cup (80 g) confectioners' sugar, plus more for garnish

¼ teaspoon cornstarch

4 croissants

5 tablespoons (40 g) sliced almonds

Seoul has an exquisitely developed breakfast pastry culture. Nearly every corner in Gangnam features a patisserie filled with rows and rows of perfectly shaped and expertly laminated croissants. But into this world, doenjang is rarely admitted. Doenjang gets rightly categorized as belonging to hansik, but wrongly confined there. Why not include it in a pastry? We know that dairy and jang are compatible. Sweet and salty, rich and creamy—when doenjang is combined with the buttery richness of a freshly baked croissant, the flavors are unforgettable. This recipe doesn't require you to go to the trouble of making a laminated dough, though—you can make it with store-bought croissants.

Preheat the oven to 350°F (180°C).

MAKE THE ALMOND CREAM: In a large bowl, whisk together the egg, salt, and rum (if using). Gradually beat in the butter and doenjang until fully incorporated.

Into another bowl, sift together the almond flour, confectioners' sugar, and cornstarch. Whisk the dry ingredients into the egg mixture until smooth and creamy.

Place the croissants on a baking sheet and divide the almond cream evenly among them, spreading it over the tops. Sprinkle evenly with the almonds. Toast the croissants in the oven for 10 to 12 minutes. Allow to cool slightly, then dust with confectioners' sugar.

DOENJANG VANILLA CRÈME BRÛLÉE
된장 바닐라 크렘 뷔렐레

SERVES 4

1 cup (240 ml) heavy cream

3 tablespoons (45 ml) whole milk

3 egg yolks

¼ cup (50 g) plus 1½ tablespoons sugar

2 teaspoons yangjo doenjang

½ vanilla bean, split lengthwise and seeds scraped out

When Mingles first opened, we didn't have a pastry chef, which left the creation of the sweet courses in the tasting menu up to me. My approach was then, and is now, to allow the desserts to live much closer to the borders of savory than the outer reaches of sweetness. It never made sense to me to abruptly end the harmonious flow of a meal with a supercharged sugary finale. Along with ganjang-glazed granola (see page 101), a gochujang-puffed grain, and a scoop of vanilla ice cream, this crème brûlée forms the jang trio that finishes the meal. The doenjang gives a subtle but appealing salty flavor, which reins in the potentially overwhelming sweetness of the brûlée.

Preheat the oven to 325°F (165°C).

In a small pot, combine the cream and milk. Cook over medium heat, stirring, until the mixture reaches 140°F (60°C), then remove from the heat and let the mixture cool to room temperature.

In a medium bowl, whisk together the egg yolks and ¼ cup (50 g) of the sugar until uniform. While whisking, slowly add the cooled cream mixture and whisk until uniform and ivory in color. Gradually whisk in the doenjang and the vanilla seeds. Pass the mixture through a coarse-mesh sieve (you want the vanilla seeds to remain).

Divide the mixture evenly among four ovenproof ramekins. Place the ramekins in a baking dish, then fill the dish with hot water to halfway up the sides of the ramekins. Transfer to the oven and bake for 50 minutes, until set. Remove from the oven and place the ramekins in the refrigerator to cool to room temperature.

When ready to serve, sprinkle the remaining 1½ tablespoons sugar evenly over the custards. Using either a kitchen torch or the broiler, heat the sugar until a thin, crisp, nut-brown layer forms over the custards. Serve immediately.

BRIE *with* DOENJANG COMPOTE

브리치즈와 된장 콤포트

SERVES 2

¼ cup (20 g) walnuts

2 teaspoons shelled pistachios

2 Brazil nuts

¼ cup (30 g) dried cranberries

1½ teaspoons blended doenjang (see page 53)

1 tablespoon rum, Cognac, or cranberry juice

1 teaspoon honey

1 wheel of Brie (preferably triple cream)

Rye bread chips, for serving

There are two ways to impress with Brie. The first is to bake it so that the heat turns the already creamy cheese even creamier. The second is to serve it with this compote, filled with warming ingredients like cranberries and roasted nuts and doenjang's added depth. Just like in the doenjang risotto on page 136, the mixture of fermented dairy product with fermented soy product is magical. Atop a half wheel of Brie or simply spread on crackers, accompanied by a glass of whiskey or wine, this compote makes the perfect snack. Keep it on hand; it is the perfect accoutrement to richer dishes like roast chicken as well.

Preheat the oven to 350°F (180°C).

Spread the walnuts, pistachios, and Brazil nuts on a baking sheet and gently toast in the oven for 2 minutes, until slightly colored. Remove from the oven (keep the oven on). Let the nuts cool slightly, then chop them and the cranberries into small pieces.

In a small bowl, mix together the doenjang, rum, and honey. Add the chopped nuts and cranberries and mix again.

Cut the Brie in half horizontally and place it, cut side up, on a parchment paper–lined baking sheet. Top each Brie half with the compote. Bake for 12 minutes, until the Brie is melted. Serve with rye bread chips on the side.

TIPS: If you don't want to serve melted Brie, you can skip the baking step. You can sprinkle more nuts on top, if you'd like.

MCGGUROOM

When Kwon Hye-Na was growing up in the early 1980s, she watched as her mother, Sung Myung-Rye, and father, Kwon Jung-Soo, tried to build their doenjang business in Cheongsong, a rural county in southeastern Korea. She watched as they laboriously spread out pebbles to form the fields for their jangdok, while they hefted and rolled the massive pots into place, while they built covered tunnels to protect the jang from the wind and harsh weather, and as together, they went through the backbreaking work of jang production. She was puzzled. At the time, most Koreans still made their own jang at home. *No one is going to buy our jang,* thought Hye-Na as a little girl. *They're going to think theirs is always better.*

But little did she know that Myung-Rye had a secret weapon. Her mother-in-law, Kim Mal-Lim, was a jang virtuoso. Already in her seventies by the 1980s, Mal-Lim had grown up the daughter-in-law of a noble family and therefore was the keeper of rare jang knowledge that flowed not from the humble traditions of halmeoni (grandmothers) but from the wealthier yangban class. Among these techniques is one called gyeopjang, a nearly extinct way of fortifying doenjang after its separation from the ganjang by the addition of fresh meju. Naturally this requires additional resources—hence both its rarity and its history as a tradition reserved for the wealthy—yet gyeopjang yields an unusually rich and flavorful doenjang. It handily sidesteps the zero-sum competition between ganjang and doenjang whereby the richer the ganjang, the weaker the doenjang. With gyeopjang, the rich just gets richer.

In her time, Mal-Lim was a passionate jang maker. While she did not sell her jang commercially, she managed to amass twenty-four jangdok that she kept behind her house in 1981. When her son and daughter-in-law decided to turn her personal jang enterprise into a business, these jangdok became the core of their collection and her techniques the heart of their new enterprise. The couple, now with two kids, decided to call their business Mcgguroom. The first syllable, *mac*, means "heritage." From the beginning, their idea was pay homage to the traditional jang-making techniques passed down from Mal-Lim. But as Hye-Na remembers, it was tough going, physically, emotionally, and financially.

For a traditional jang artisan, like for a whiskey distiller, there is a long and difficult gestational period during which the first products must age before they come to market and, hopefully, turn a profit. For two years, the family waited while their doenjang aged. That's two years not knowing whether the gamble would pay off, two years of no income. As Hye-Na recalls, her grandmother helped her mother tend to the jangdok. She insisted that Mcgguroom use only domestic, and ideally locally grown, soybeans of the highest quality. Gyeopjang is especially labor-intensive. After the traditional separation of ganjang and doenjang, the artisan must break up additional meju and add it to the ganjang to restore the proper richness, which allows for a secondary fermentation. At Mcgguroom, this secondary fermentation lasts eighteen months. It is a slow process, but one that allows an even richer bacterial profile to develop. Hye-Na remembers her parents selling their doenjang in small street markets in the county. Slowly the word spread that Mcgguroom was producing some of the best doenjang in the area. By 1989, Myung-Rye and her husband had applied for a business license, and Mcgguroom was (officially, at least) born.

Today the Mcgguroom factory sits nestled in a gentle valley like a jang maker's paradise. In 2018, the family built a graceful traditional Korean house called a hanok. With its traditional tile roof, white walls, and pine woodwork, the hanok is surrounded by cracked and otherwise unusable inverted jangdok. Unlike hanok in the colder northern regions, which are built as squares with a central courtyard, this one is built as an L, a shape that allows cool air to flow through the rooms during the summer. The hanok, where Hye-Na lives with her mother, father, and daughter, sits on a hill. Beneath it is a modern café, reception area, and store, built in 2018, adjacent to a small parking lot.

Behind all this is the production facility, a short walk away but closed to visitors, where Hye-Na, Myung-Rye, and seventeen other employees now work. The original twenty-four jangdok have swollen to nearly 3,200, which sit in seven covered tunnels. Myung-Rye has relentlessly updated the facility while still preserving the traditional aspects of jang making. Today state-of-the-art packaging equipment, vacuum sealers, meju-molding machines, and X-ray detectors occupy the modern factory. Meju are aged in specially designed temperature-controlled rooms. Gamasot have been replaced by industrial steamers. But push open the door to the jangdokdae, and it's as if you've stepped back in time.

At seventy-five years old, Myung-Rye's hands are still near wrinkle-free, the result, she says, of plunging them into doenjang for years. She wears a long apron over a dress and slippers. Myung-Rye is still the master artisan, but Hye-Na is learning the craft, too. Mcgguroom, perhaps better than any other producer, embodies how jang making is a tradition passed down through the generations by women. Often this transmission is from mother-in-law to daughter-in-law; sometimes, as in this case, it's directly from mother to daughter.

The reason for this is the unique, and vexed, role a daughter-in-law plays in the heavily patriarchal Korean society. Dating from sixth-century BCE Confucian ideals, and long embedded in familial structures, is the idea that a woman, once married, joins her husband's household, whereas a man, once married, becomes the head of his parents' household. (This applies to the eldest son; younger sons and their families frequently move out but live nearby.) It is through the son that familial lineage passes and to the son great benefits flow from birth. Traditionally it is said that mothers pass on flesh to their children whereas fathers pass on bone. Since bone lasts longer than flesh, it is only through the males that clan membership can be passed. Daughters, on the other hand, have been seen as only transient residents of their birth homes. As soon as a woman is wed, she becomes in some ways a handmaiden to her mother-in-law. Clearly this presents a range of issues, particularly salient today. And though legally this system was weakened by the New Civil Code of 1958, which abolished rules surrounding the head

of household, it remains embedded in all levels of Korean society. It helps to explain why, for instance, Myung-Rye learned how to make jang from Mal-Lim. Modernity helps explain why it is Hye-Na, not her sister-in-law, who helps run Mcgguroom.

In today's more modern urban and industrialized society, the mores of the past are being weakened. As any Korean daughter-in-law will tell you, there is still an enormous pressure felt when entering into an in-law relationship. The old saying that a bride must be "three years deaf, three years dumb, and three years blind" still holds largely true. But at the same time, sons are no longer staying home, and daughters are no longer entering their husbands' households. So, whereas a generation ago, jang making was primarily passed from mother-in-law to daughter-in-law, it's becoming more common, as at Mcgguroom, for the lineage to run from mother to daughter directly.

What makes the labor-intensive work worth it, Hye-Na says, is the jang itself and seeing her family's long tradition continue. From simply the best jang in the valley, the result of one woman's passion and knowledge, Mcgguroom today turns out 110 metric tons of doenjang, 100 metric tons of ganjang, and 25 metric tons of gochujang every year. Their product is shipped around the world, converting jang neophytes and delighting jang experts. Combining modern marketing, technology, and logistical prowess, these aged earth-toned jangdok hold not just jang but, in many ways, the future of jang as well.

GOCHUJANG

CUCUMBER MUCHIM
오이무침

SERVES 2

3 small cucumbers, cut into ¼-inch (6 mm) chunks

½ teaspoon kosher salt

2 teaspoons sugar

1½ teaspoons brown rice vinegar

1¼ teaspoons gochujang

1 teaspoon coarsely ground gochugaru

1 teaspoon hansik ganjang

¼ onion, thinly sliced

Sesame seeds, for garnish

This slightly spicy, very bright banchan is found on almost every Korean table. *Muchim* means "mixed with seasoning," which in this case is a bracing combination of salty, spicy, and sweet. The most common vegetable by far for muchim is cucumber. Refreshing and plentiful during the summer, cucumber is supplanted by radish during the winter. Both absorb the seasoning well and are the rare vegetables that can, in a pinch, substitute for kimchi. (The flavors of a muchim mimic those of a quick kimchi.)

In a bowl, gently toss the cucumber with the salt and set aside for 30 minutes. Quickly rinse the cucumber with water and squeeze in towels to remove the moisture.

In a medium bowl, combine the sugar, vinegar, gochujang, gochugaru, and ganjang and mix well. Add the cucumbers and onion and toss to combine. Sprinkle with sesame seeds and serve immediately.

TIP: This muchim is best eaten right away but can be stored in an airtight container in the refrigerator for up to 2 days.

MYEOLCHI BOKKEUM 멸치볶음
Stir-Fried Dried Anchovies

SERVES 4

⅔ cup (60 g) walnuts, halved or quartered

2 cups (100 g) medium or small dried anchovies

2 tablespoons neutral oil, such as grapeseed or canola

1 tablespoon finely chopped green onion, white parts only

1 garlic clove, finely chopped

2 teaspoons coarsely ground gochugaru

3½ tablespoons (60 g) sauté gochujang (see page 54)

1 tablespoon honey

¼ teaspoon sesame seeds

Korea is a peninsula, so it makes sense that dried anchovies—and anchovies in general—are part of the gamchilmat-rich underpainting of hansik. After the anchovies are caught, they are steamed and dried. Often they are made into a broth (see page 50), but frequently they appear in banchan, too, often paired with nuts like walnuts or almonds. The key is to mitigate the fishiness of the anchovy, which is done by making sure the head, backbone, and guts are removed and that the fish are completely dry before you begin cooking. The appeal is in the texture as much as the flavor. This is a rare crunchy banchan, and though you can keep it in the refrigerator for up to a week, it's best when eaten right away.

Preheat the oven to 350°F (180°C).

Spread the walnuts on a baking sheet and toast in the oven for about 5 minutes, until lightly browned and fragrant. Remove and set aside.

Meanwhile, remove the anchovy heads, backbones, and guts and split the anchovies in half (if you are using small anchovies, you can skip this process). Microwave the anchovies on a plate for 30 to 60 seconds to make sure they are completely dry. (Alternatively, stir-fry the anchovies lightly in a dry pan over low heat.)

In a generous-size pan, combine the oil, green onion, and garlic and heat over low heat until the oil is shimmering but not bubbling. Add the gochugaru and mix well. Cook for a few minutes to infuse the oil, then add the gochujang, honey, and ¼ cup (60 ml) water to the pan. Bring the mixture to a boil, then add the anchovies. Add the walnuts and stir well. Cook for 2 to 3 minutes, then remove the anchovies and spread them on a large tray to cool. Toss with the sesame seeds and serve immediately.

CRUDITÉS *with* KOREAN RANCH SAUCE

고추장 랜치 소스와 신선한 채소

SERVES 4

FOR THE KOREAN RANCH

½ cup (125 g) mayonnaise

2½ tablespoons gochujang

4 teaspoons fresh lemon juice

2 garlic cloves, minced

1 teaspoon kosher salt

2 asparagus stalks, trimmed

10 green beans

1 small cucumber, cut into 2-inch (5 cm) batons

½ large carrot, cut into 2-inch (5 cm) batons

1 celery stalk, cut into 2-inch (5 cm) batons

2 radishes, greens removed, quartered or halved

1 medium tomato, cut into sixths

8 cherry tomatoes

2 mini bell peppers, halved and seeded

⅛ zucchini, cut into 2-inch (5 cm) pieces

1½ teaspoons extra-virgin olive oil

Gochujang powder (see page 48; optional)

Most anju (drinking snacks) are fried or salty. And though I love them, sometimes I want something at least vaguely healthier. That's the idea behind this simple hors d'oeuvre. The veggies are healthy, crunchy, and sweet, but it's the gochujang-spiced aioli that makes this the world's greatest dip. Nothing is more satisfying than the crunch and spice of these crudités followed by a long sip of Cass, the Korean equivalent of Natty Ice.

MAKE THE KOREAN RANCH: In a small bowl, mix together the mayonnaise, gochujang, lemon juice, and garlic. Set aside.

In a medium pot, combine 4¼ cups (1 L) water and the salt and bring to a boil over high heat. Fill a large bowl with equal parts ice and cold water.

Blanch the asparagus and green beans in the boiling water for 3 to 4 minutes, then transfer to the ice bath immediately to stop the cooking. Once cool, remove the vegetables, pat dry, and trim into 2-inch (5 cm) pieces.

Place the vegetables on a serving platter. Sprinkle with the olive oil and gochujang powder, if desired. Serve the Korean ranch alongside the vegetables.

TIP: The Korean ranch will keep, covered, in the refrigerator for up to 1 week.

GOCHUJANG JJIGAE 고추장찌개
Gochujang Stew

SERVES 4

⅔ cup plus 3 tablespoons (250 g) gochujang

3 tablespoons plus 1 teaspoon (45 ml) hansik ganjang

3 tablespoons (50 g) yangjo doenjang

2½ tablespoons coarsely ground gochugaru

4¼ cups (1 L) anchovy stock (see page 50)

2½ cups (200 g) peeled and diced daikon radish (1-inch/2.5 cm dice)

18 ounces (500 g) pork shoulder, cut into 1-inch (2.5 cm) cubes

1 large potato, cut into 1-inch (2.5 cm) dice

1 zucchini, cut into 1-inch (2.5 cm) dice

2 pyogo (shiitake) mushrooms, quartered

3 green onions, cut diagonally into ⅓-inch (0.75 cm) pieces

4 garlic cloves, finely chopped

4 cups (800 g) cooked rice, for serving

The Inuit living in Canada's Nunavik region have more than fifty words for snow. Koreans have nearly as many for soup. That should give you an idea of how important soup is to our culture, essentially one based on wringing as much sustenance from a protein as possible. There are guks, tangs, jjigaes, jeongols, and more. *Jjigae* might best be translated as "thickened stew." When the sauce is thickened with jang, the broth itself becomes nourishing while also penetrating the vegetables with deep, sustaining, comforting flavor. As with most stews, this one grows more delicious in the days after it's made, when the flavors have had time to intermingle.

In a small bowl, mix together the gochujang, ganjang, doenjang, and gochugaru.

In a large pot, combine the stock, the jang mixture, and 4¼ cups (1 L) water and mix well. Add the daikon and bring the mixture to a boil over medium heat. Boil for 5 minutes, then add the pork and potato and cook, stirring often, for 5 minutes more. Add the zucchini and mushrooms and cook for 10 minutes, until the pork is cooked through and opaque throughout, then add the green onions and garlic. Allow the stew to boil for 1 minute more, then serve immediately with a side of rice.

Leftover stew can be stored in an airtight container in the refrigerator for up to 2 days.

DAKBOKKEUMTANG 닭볶음탕
Spicy Chicken Stew

1 (2½-pound/1 kg) whole chicken, cut into 12 pieces

½ cup (120 ml) dark mat-ganjang (see page 53)

2 tablespoons coarsely ground gochugaru

1 tablespoon gochujang

1 tablespoon sugar

1 teaspoon hansik ganjang

2 garlic cloves, chopped

½ teaspoon chopped fresh ginger

1 small potato, quartered, or 6 fingerling potatoes

½ medium onion, quartered

3 green onions, sliced into 1-inch (2.5 cm) pieces

2 red chiles, thinly sliced

4 cups (800 g) cooked rice, for serving

Korean summers get hot, very hot, and the dog days—the hottest—which take place usually in July or August, are call sambok. *Bok* means to lie down or give up—these are days when you just can't *even*. Westerners might seek relief in ice cream or paletas, but we go in the opposite direction. According to Korean wellness traditions, known as hanbang, you should eat *hot* foods on hot days. As the idiom goes, fight fire with fire. The hotter the day, the hotter the food. (And conversely, the colder the day, the colder the food.)

These days, during sambok, most Koreans enjoy samgyetang, a chicken soup made with ginseng, rice, and jujube. But I prefer this spicy chicken stew instead. Either way, the idea is that the hot chicken invigorates your body, giving you the much-needed energy to escape heat-induced malaise. Think of this soup like Korean coq au vin. The red wine is replaced with the ganjang and gochujang, whose flavors permeate the meat.

Bring a large pot of water to a boil over high heat. Rinse the chicken pieces well. Blanch the chicken in the boiling water for 1 minute, then remove it and let dry.

In a small bowl, mix together the mat-ganjang, gochugaru, gochujang, sugar, ganjang, garlic, and ginger.

In a large pot, combine the ganjang mixture and 2¼ cups (500 ml) water and mix well. Add the chicken and bring to a boil over high heat. Reduce the heat to low and cook for 20 minutes, then add the potato and onion and cook until the vegetables are tender and the chicken is cooked through, about 20 minutes. Add the green onions and chiles. Increase the heat to high and bring the soup back to a boil, then remove from the heat and let sit for 10 minutes before serving.

Serve with the rice. Leftover soup can be stored in an airtight container in the refrigerator for up to 2 days.

YANGNYEOM CHICKEN 한국식 양념치킨
Korean Fried Chicken

SERVES 4

FOR THE BRINED CHICKEN

1½ teaspoons coarsely ground gochugaru

1½ teaspoons kosher salt

1 teaspoon sugar

½ teaspoon yangjo ganjang

Four 6-ounce (180 g) boneless, skin-on chicken thighs

FOR THE SAUCE

6 tablespoons (90 ml) rice syrup

3 tablespoons plus 2¼ teaspoons (45 g) sugar

3 tablespoons (50 g) gochujang

3 tablespoons (45 ml) yangjo ganjang

2½ tablespoons rice vinegar

3 garlic cloves, finely chopped

2 green Cheongyang chiles or jalapeños, thinly sliced

FOR FRYING AND FINISHING

9 cups (2.2 L) neutral oil, such as grapeseed or canola

2 cups (200 g) frying batter mix (see page 47)

2 tablespoons crushed roasted peanuts

1 green onion, white part only, sliced into thin strips

Embedded in the history of Korean fried chicken is the history of Korea in the twentieth century. First introduced by Black American GIs stationed in Korea during the 6-2-5 War, fried chicken has grown into a national obsession. What was once rare—even the affordable chicken was once out of reach of most Koreans, and cooking oil was too precious for deep-frying—has become one of our greatest culinary exports. Crunchy, salty, and sweet, Korean fried chicken is the most common anju, a genre of food (often fried) that is consumed while drinking. In fact, fried chicken goes by many names, one of which is chimaek, a portmanteau of *chikin*, meaning fried chicken, and *maekju*, beer. My favorite nickname for fried chicken, however, is Chisus—"chicken Jesus." That gives you an idea of how revered fried chicken is in South Korea.

There are two types of fried chicken. A simpler version with a light golden crust is called huraideu, while this version, doused in a complex sauce made of gochujang, ganjang, and many spices, is called yangnyeom. Both types rely on a long brine to imbue the meat with juiciness, cornstarch to create its crystalline crust, and double frying for maximum crunchiness. Gochujang plays a pivotal role in this recipe; the chicken gets tossed in a spicy gochujang sauce after frying to add an irresistible coating.

BRINE THE CHICKEN: In a large nonreactive container, combine the gochugaru, salt, sugar, ganjang, and 1⅔ cups (400 ml) water and mix well. Submerge the chicken thighs in the brine, cover, and refrigerate for 12 hours.

MAKE THE SAUCE: In a small pot, combine the rice syrup, sugar, gochujang, ganjang, and vinegar and bring to a boil over high heat. Remove from the heat and let cool to room temperature, then stir in the garlic and chiles and set aside.

FRY THE CHICKEN: Remove the chicken from the brine and let it come to room temperature. Chop the chicken into 1-inch (2.5 cm) cubes.

Fill a large skillet with oil to a depth of at least 2 inches (5 cm; it should be deep enough to fully submerge the chicken) and heat the oil over high heat to 350°F (170°C). Line a tray with paper towels.

recipe continues

Meanwhile, in a bowl, whisk together 1⅓ cups (130 g) of the frying batter mix and 1 cup plus 1 tablespoon (260 ml) cold water to form a wet batter. Pass the batter through a sieve, if desired, to make sure there are no lumps. Place the remaining ⅔ cup (70 g) dry batter mix on a plate.

Add the chicken to the batter and turn until well coated. Working in batches, dip the battered chicken pieces in the dry mix to coat, then add them to the hot oil, making sure they do not touch and without crowding the pan. Cook for 2½ minutes, or until golden brown. Transfer to the prepared tray and let the oil come back up to 350°F (170°C) before cooking the next batch. Repeat until all the chicken has been fried.

Once all the chicken has been fried a first time, fry it again, starting with the first pieces you fried, for 2½ to 3 minutes, until extra crispy. Drain again on the paper towels. (This resting and refrying is a very important process for crispy and juicy fried chicken.)

To serve, gently toss the fried chicken with the gochujang sauce, being careful not to disturb the breading. Top with the crushed peanuts and green onion to finish.

KIMCHI BOKKEUMBAP *and* BAEK KIMCHI COLESLAW 김치볶음밥과 백김치 코울슬로

Kimchi Fried Rice with White Kimchi Coleslaw

SERVES 2

FOR THE COLESLAW

1 cup (50 g) thinly sliced cabbage

2¼ teaspoons brown rice vinegar

½ teaspoon sugar

¼ teaspoon kosher salt (or 3% of the cabbage's weight)

¼ cup (50 g) white kimchi, thinly sliced

FOR THE FRIED RICE

2 eggs

2 cups (400 g) cold cooked rice

1 tablespoon sauté gochujang (see page 54)

1 teaspoon yangjo ganjang

1 tablespoon canola oil

5½ ounces (160 g) bacon (about three ¼-inch/6 mm slices), sliced into ¼-inch (6 mm) strips

4 green onions, white parts only, coarsely chopped

¼ medium onion, cut into ¼-inch (6 mm) dice

2 garlic cloves, coarsely chopped

1 cup (200 g) cabbage kimchi, sliced into ¼-inch (6 mm) strips

2 tablespoons perilla oil

Sesame seeds, for garnish

Kimchi fried rice was my gateway recipe into cooking. Until I was around seven years old, I had never cooked for myself. My mom was a good cook and made all the meals for my father, my younger brother, and me. One day, though, I went to my friend's house; his mother had a job outside the home and so he often cooked for himself. He made me kimchi fried rice, and I was impressed. The next time my mom went out with her friends, I asked if I could make dinner. Surprisingly, she agreed.

The core ingredients for kimchi fried rice—kimchi, leftover rice, and eggs—are ones that almost every Korean household always has on hand. Not wanting, even then, to be derivative of my friend, I used dried noodles (guksu) instead of rice. My recipe was not a success. It didn't matter; I was hooked. (My younger brother, who had no choice but to eat my experiment, was less enthused.) I begged my mom to buy me cookbooks. I began watching cooking documentaries and reading cooking comic books. As I got older, my kimchi fried rice got better, too. The gochujang was an addition I learned from my dad; kimchi fried rice was one of the few things he cooked, too. I love how the sharpness of the kimchi and the spicy sweetness of the gochujang interact.

I haven't stopped improving the recipe. When I was living in the States, I became obsessed with the milky-white coleslaw sold at KFC. I began adding it to my own kimchi fried rice and soon made my own coleslaw, mixing it with white—or unspiced—kimchi as the base. Other variations, like the addition of basil pesto, I learned from my friends Kwang Uh and Mina Park at Baroo in Los Angeles. As it turns out, for many Korean and Korean American chefs, kimchi fried rice was one of their earliest projects and one that they keep on improving, too.

MAKE THE COLESLAW: In a large bowl, mix together the cabbage, vinegar, sugar, salt, and 1 teaspoon water. Let the mixture rest for 30 minutes, then squeeze out the moisture and mix in the white kimchi. Cover and refrigerate until ready to use.

MAKE THE FRIED RICE: Beat the eggs in a medium bowl, then add the rice and mix well. Let sit for 20 minutes so the egg soaks into the rice.

recipe continues

Meanwhile, in a small bowl, mix together the gochujang and ganjang and set aside.

In a large pan, heat the canola oil over high heat until shimmering. Add the bacon, green onions, onion, and garlic and cook until the bacon is crispy and the onions are translucent, 4 to 5 minutes. Add the cabbage kimchi and stir well, then add the jang mixture. Cook for 1 minute. Reduce the heat to medium and add the rice. Cook, stirring continuously so the rice does not stick, for 5 minutes, until each grain of rice is thoroughly coated with the jang mixture. Add the perilla oil and toss the rice again so each grain is coated.

To serve, divide the rice evenly between two plates and top with sesame seeds. Serve with a side of the white kimchi coleslaw.

YUKHWE BIBIMBAP 육회 비빔밥
Beef Tartare Bibimbap

SERVES 2

5½ ounces (160 g) high-quality beef sirloin

1 teaspoon kosher salt

½ cup (60 g) soybean or mung bean sprouts

½ teaspoon hansik ganjang

½ teaspoon perilla oil

FOR THE GOCHUJANG SAUCE

⅓ cup (90 g) gochujang

3 tablespoons (45 ml) perilla oil

¼ Korean (Asian) pear, peeled and cored

1 tablespoon plus 1 teaspoon sugar

1 teaspoon yangjo ganjang

Pinch of freshly ground black pepper

2 teaspoons sesame seeds, finely ground

2 garlic cloves, minced

2 cups (400 g) cooked rice

10 perilla leaves, thinly sliced

6 or 7 butter lettuce leaves, thinly sliced

2 egg yolks

1½ teaspoons pine nuts (about 20)

½ teaspoon sesame seeds

1 tablespoon perilla oil

The closest analog to yukhwe in Western cuisine is steak tartare. Yukhwe is raw meat, often, but not necessarily, beef. That's where the similarity ends. Whereas in a bistro-style tartare the meat is made sharp with the addition of capers, alliums, and Worcestershire sauce, yukhwe is turned Technicolor, sweet, and spicy with the addition of bright gochujang, Korean pear (sweeter than its American cousin), sesame oil, and pine nuts.

Like many things hansik, the story of yukhwe is both ancient and modern. Recipes for yukhwe have been recorded since the seventeenth century, when it was mentioned as food for the royal court of the Joseon dynasty. It wasn't until beef became more widely available in the twentieth century that the dish proliferated. Now there are many regional variations, though the most famous is that of Jinju, a city in the southern tip of Korea with a famous beef market. Though gochujang is rarely paired with cooked beef, the flavor profile is perfect for its raw form. The dish can be made even better if accompanied by leafy greens and rice, which turns it into a bibimbap, as it is here.

NOTE: You'll be eating raw beef in this dish, so be sure to use the highest quality. Ask your favorite butcher for their freshest sirloin.

Place the beef in the freezer for 1 hour to make it easier to cut. Once slightly frozen, remove it and cut it into thin 2-inch-long (5 cm) slices.

In a medium pot, combine 4¼ cups (1 L) water and the salt and bring to a boil over high heat. Fill a medium bowl with equal parts ice and cold water.

Rinse the bean sprouts, then remove any rotten parts and bean hulls. Blanch the bean sprouts in the boiling water for 1 to 2 minutes (the sprouts should not lose their crunchiness), then transfer to the ice bath immediately to stop the cooking. Drain the bean sprouts and toss them with the hansik ganjang and perilla oil.

MAKE THE SAUCE: In a blender, combine the gochujang, perilla oil, pear, sugar, yangjo ganjang, and pepper and blend well. Fold in the

sesame seeds and garlic by hand. Pour 2 tablespoons of the sauce over the beef and toss well; add more sauce to taste, if you like.

Divide the rice evenly between two bowls. Top evenly with the perilla leaves, lettuce, and bean sprouts, then with the tartare. Make a small indentation in the meat and carefully add an egg yolk to each serving. Finish each bowl with half the pine nuts, sesame seeds, and perilla oil. Serve additional sauce on the side and have your guests add to taste.

KIMCHI BIBIM GUKSU 김치비빔국수
Kimchi Mixed Noodles with Gochujang Sauce

SERVES 2

2 eggs

FOR THE SAUCE

¾ cup (225 g)
chogochujang (see page 54)

2½ tablespoons honey

2 tablespoons plus
1 teaspoon hansik
ganjang

¼ Korean (Asian) pear or
apple, cored

⅛ medium onion

1 garlic clove, peeled

3 tablespoons (25 g)
coarsely ground
gochugaru

Kosher salt

5 ounces (140 g) somyeon
(Korean wheat noodles)

½ cup (100 g) sliced
cabbage kimchi (½-inch/
1 cm slices)

¼ medium cucumber,
thinly sliced

1 teaspoon perilla oil

Sesame seeds

Bibim guksu is a cold noodle dish—similar to naengmyeon and kongguksu—that is a perfect meal for a hot summer day. This recipe is one of the most classic and well-known in Korea and it's easy to see why. Not only are most of the ingredients staples that we have on hand at any given time, but it's fast and easy to make. The spiciness of gochujang, the sharpness of chogochujang, the sourness and texture of the cabbage kimchi, and the sweetness from the honey and pear hold each other in perfect harmonious balance. The sauce, meanwhile, is so good that you can use it for dipping everything from pork belly (see page 139) to a simple bibimbap with some raw vegetables. This recipe makes enough for a few meals; it keeps in the refrigerator for up to 2 weeks.

Place the eggs in a small pot, cover with cold water, and bring to a boil over high heat. Boil the eggs for 9 minutes (or 8, if you want a creamier yolk), then remove and rinse under cold water. Peel the eggs and cut in half; set aside.

MAKE THE SAUCE: In a blender, combine the chogochujang, honey, ganjang, pear, onion, and garlic and blend well. Stir in the gochugaru by hand until incorporated. Set aside.

Bring 8⅓ cups (2 L) lightly salted water to a boil in a large pot over high heat. Fill a bowl with equal parts ice and water. Add the noodles to the boiling water and cook for about 4 minutes (cooking times vary by brand, so check the packaging). Quickly drain the noodles in a sieve, then set the sieve in the ice bath and let cool completely.

In a small bowl, mix 1 tablespoon of the sauce with the kimchi. In a large bowl, mix the noodles with ⅓ cup (80 ml) of the sauce, then divide them evenly between two bowls. Top each evenly with the cucumber, the seasoned kimchi, and a halved soft-boiled egg. Finish with a drizzle of perilla oil and a sprinkle of sesame seeds.

SEAFOOD PLATTER *with* GOCHUJANG SALSA *and* GOCHUJANG COCKTAIL SAUCE

고추장 살사와 고추장 칵테일 소스를 곁들인 해산물 플래터

SERVES 4

½ cup (75 g) kosher salt

3½ tablespoons (50 ml) white wine vinegar

1 bay leaf

5 whole white peppercorns

1 or 2 fresh lobsters

8 to 12 jumbo shrimp, deveined and rinsed with cold water

8 oysters

4 scallops, in the shell

FOR THE GOCHUJANG SALSA

2 tablespoons plus ¾ teaspoon extra-virgin olive oil

2 tablespoons fresh lemon juice

2 tablespoons chogochujang (see page 54)

1½ teaspoons hot sauce

⅓ small tomato, diced

½ celery stalk, diced

⅙ red onion, diced

½ Cheongyang chile or jalapeño, finely diced

FOR THE CHOGOCHUJANG COCKTAIL SAUCE

½ cup (120 ml) ketchup

¼ cup (65 g) chogochujang (see page 54)

1 tablespoon plus 1 teaspoon fresh lemon juice

Chogochujang (or chojang, as it is frequently written) is magical with seafood, especially raw seafood. With briny bivalves, like oysters, clams, and scallops, the vinegar-tinged spiciness of the chogochujang accents the flavors of the ocean, like a deeper dash of Tabasco. The onion, tomato, and celery turn this from a sauce into a salsa and function to broaden and soften the chojang, which can be overbearing when consumed straight with no chaser. With sweeter crustaceans like shrimp, prawns, and lobster, I prefer the horseradishy flavor of the chogochujang cocktail sauce, which is even easier to make and always a hit at my home. The bracing green plum mignonette complements both sweet and briny sea creatures.

Bring 12½ cups (3 L) water to a boil in a large pot over high heat and add the salt, vinegar, bay leaf, and peppercorns. Fill a large bowl with equal parts ice and cold water.

When the water boils, turn off the heat and quickly add the lobsters. Cover with a lid and steam for 12 minutes. Transfer the lobsters to the ice bath (reserving the water in the pot) and let cool. Using a large sharp knife, cut the body of each lobster in half lengthwise. Break off the claws and knuckles and pick out the meat, setting it aside in a bowl as you work.

Place the shrimp in the reserved lobster cooking water, bring to a boil over high heat, and cook for 2 to 3 minutes, until opaque. Chill the shrimp in the ice bath (add more ice if needed to keep the water cold) to stop the cooking and set aside.

Shuck the oysters by inserting a thin sharp knife, ideally an oyster knife, in the back hinge of each oyster, then rotating it 90 degrees, until the oyster cracks open. Wipe off the knife and then reinsert it along the upper (flatter) shell of the oyster to cut the muscle holding the meat to the shell. Remove the top half of the shell, then insert the knife between the oyster and the bottom shell to cut the other muscle holding it to the shell. Set aside.

To open each scallop, insert a thin knife between the shells and run it backward from the mouth to the hinge. Remove the scallop's frill, stomach contents, and coral (if desired). Rinse the scallop well

1 tablespoon grated fresh or prepared horseradish

1 garlic clove, chopped

¼ teaspoon hot sauce

FOR THE GREEN PLUM MIGNONETTE SAUCE

1 shallot, finely chopped

2 tablespoons green plum vinegar, sherry vinegar, or white wine vinegar

1 tablespoon plus 2 teaspoons toasted sesame oil

1 tablespoon plus 2 teaspoons yangjo ganjang

1 tablespoon plus 2 teaspoons maesil-cheong (green plum syrup)

1 tablespoon plus ½ teaspoon fresh lime juice

½ teaspoon whole black peppercorns, crushed

TO ASSEMBLE

Coarse salt (optional)

½ lemon

½ lime

in salted cold water, then slice horizontally into 3 or 4 thin pieces. Repeat with the remaining scallops. Set aside.

MAKE THE SALSA: In a medium bowl, mix together the olive oil, lemon juice, chogochujang, and hot sauce. Add the tomato, celery, onion, and chile and mix well; set aside.

MAKE THE COCKTAIL SAUCE: In a small bowl, mix together the ketchup, chogochujang, lemon juice, horseradish, garlic, and hot sauce until well combined.

MAKE THE MIGNONETTE: In a small bowl, mix together the shallot, vinegar, sesame oil, ganjang, maesil-cheong, lime juice, and crushed peppercorns.

ASSEMBLE THE SEAFOOD PLATTER: Place ice (or coarse salt) in a wide shallow bowl and arrange the prepared seafood atop it. Rinse the lemon and lime, then cut them into wedges and place them around the seafood. Serve the three sauces in ramekins alongside.

GOCHUJANG HWE MUCHIM 고추장 회무침
Snapper Crudo with Chogochujang Dressing

SERVES 2

4 to 5 ounces (120 to 140 g) sashimi-grade snapper fillet or high-quality salmon

Kosher salt

3½ tablespoons (60 g) chogochujang (see page 54)

2 teaspoons toasted sesame oil

½ teaspoon coarsely ground gochugaru

1 napa cabbage leaf, cut into ¼-inch-thick (6 mm) slices

¼ small onion, cut into ¼-inch-thick (6 mm) slices

½ cup (30 g) chopped minari (water dropwort; 1-inch-long/2.5 cm pieces)

12 perilla leaves

1 garlic clove, thinly sliced

1 tablespoon sesame seeds

The delicate sweetness of silky raw fish is what makes hwe (crudo) such a refreshing starter. In Western cuisine, this quality is counterbalanced by acid in some form, usually citrus, and underscored by the sweetness of olive oil, and perked up by an element of heat (thinly sliced chiles) and, of course, salt. Chogochujang manages to combine all of these flavors into one ingredient. Salty, spicy, sweet, and acidic, chogochujang is like an Instagram filter: It beautifies the fish without completely obscuring it. (It works just as well with lightly cooked oysters, shrimp, or scallops.) As for the rest of the elements of this muchim, the perilla and minari in particular add a strong herbaceousness that can withstand the chogochujang.

Remove the skin from the snapper, if needed, and rinse the fillets well in salted cold water. Using a paper towel, blot the fillets dry and then slice them as thinly as possible with a very sharp knife and place on a platter. Cover and refrigerate until chilled.

Meanwhile, in a small bowl, whisk together 2 tablespoons of the chogochujang, the sesame oil, and the gochugaru until incorporated. Add the napa cabbage, onion, and minari. Gently mix with your hands or chopsticks until each element is well coated.

Evenly divide the remaining 1½ tablespoons chogochujang atop the slices of chilled fish. Roll up the slices of fish and place them on a platter beside the perilla leaves, vegetables, and garlic. Finish with the sesame seeds and serve immediately.

SEARED SCALLOPS *with* SPICY SPINACH SALAD
고추장 소스를 곁들인 구운 관자와 시금치 샐러드

SERVES 2

2 small radishes, thinly sliced on a mandoline

3 teaspoons extra-virgin olive oil

5 or 6 large (U12) scallops

1 ounce (30 g) baby spinach leaves, washed and dried

1½ tablespoons chogochujang (see page 54)

1 small cucumber, thinly sliced lengthwise on a mandoline

Zest and juice of ½ lemon

Pinch of sesame seeds (optional)

The magic of chogochujang is that its spicy acidity and sweet salinity play perfectly with crustaceans. Originally a dipping sauce (see page 54), or one drizzled like a mignonette, chogochujang can also be made into more of a vinaigrette with the addition of olive oil and lemon. These ingredients act as a bridge between traditional hansik elements and Western ones, such as spinach. If you don't have spinach, this starter works equally well with other leafy greens like frisée or butter lettuce.

In a small bowl, soak the radishes in cold water to make the slices translucent and crisp.

Meanwhile, in a large skillet, heat 1½ teaspoons of the olive oil over medium heat until shimmering. Add the scallops and sear, undisturbed, for 1 to 2 minutes, until golden brown on the bottom. Turn off the heat, flip the scallops, and let them cook for 30 to 60 seconds in the residual heat. Transfer the scallops to a sheet of parchment paper and set aside.

To serve, place the spinach on a platter and drizzle the chogochujang evenly over the top. Spread some radish slices on top of the spinach, then drape the cucumber over the top. Place the seared scallops on top. Drizzle with the remaining 1½ teaspoons olive oil and finish with the lemon zest, lemon juice, and sesame seeds, if desired.

GOCHUJANG BBQ COOKOUT

캠핑용 고추장 바베큐

SERVES 3 OR 4

1 cup (300 g) BBQ
gochujang (see page 55)

1 tablespoon canola oil,
plus more as needed

4 (9-ounce/250 g) bone-in
pork chops, about 1½ inches
(4 cm) thick

Leaves from 7 sage sprigs

8 asparagus stalks,
trimmed and peeled

2 small onions, cut into
¾-inch-thick (2 cm) rings

Salt and freshly ground
black pepper

8 to 12 jumbo shrimp,
deveined

8 oysters

2 lemons, halved

1 lime, halved

The first year I lived in America, one of my colleagues in West Palm Beach invited me to his house for an outdoor barbecue. I think it might have been out of pity—I knew literally no one in the city—but I was excited to go regardless. I had heard of American barbecues with their endless supply of hot dogs, cheeseburgers, beers, slip-and-slides, and lawn chairs, but I had never been to one. In Korea, we do have barbecue grill culture, but of the indoor tabletop kind.

The party did not disappoint. It was as American a meal as I think I've ever had, or ever will. We circled around the grill, watching meat cook, and though I hardly said a word (or understood much), I got a glimpse of the wonderful, almost primal camaraderie of the American barbecue. When I left Florida a year later, destined for Spain, I invited my colleagues over to my place for a farewell cookout. They were mostly a bunch of chefs, so I wanted to impress them. Instead of the standard fare, I cooked marinated pork ribs and short ribs, shrimp, and oysters on my charcoal grill. They were, I think, impressed and intrigued, and I left Florida with the confidence of a man in a novelty apron, holding his spatula like a scepter before a smoking grill.

NOTE: Like most marinades, this one takes time. The pork chops should be marinated for 12 hours before grilling.

In a bowl, whisk together the BBQ gochujang and canola oil. Set aside ⅓ cup (100 g) in a separate small bowl.

Pat the pork chops dry with a paper towel. Place them on a plate and rub them with the sage leaves. Brush them evenly with the larger portion of the gochujang sauce. Cover and marinate in the refrigerator for 12 to 24 hours.

Allow the meat to come to room temperature for 30 minutes to 1 hour before grilling. Preheat a charcoal grill to high.

Place the pork on the grill and brush with the leftover marinade from the plate. Grill, turning the pork every 30 to 60 seconds to avoid charring, for 10 minutes or so, until the internal temperature reaches 160°F (70°C), then transfer to a plate to rest for 5 minutes.

Place the asparagus and onions on a tray and season with salt and pepper. Drizzle with canola oil and toss to coat. Grill until charred, about 7 minutes.

recipe continues

Meanwhile, rinse the shrimp and oysters under cold running water to remove any dirt or grit. Grill the shrimp, cut side down, brushing the reserved ⅓ cup (100 g) gochujang sauce over their opened backs, until opaque, 3 to 4 minutes. Remove and set aside. Grill the oysters until their shells begin to pop open, 5 to 7 minutes, then carefully remove them from the grill and pry the shells open. Brush the oysters with sauce as well and return to the grill for a minute or so, then remove. Place the lemon and lime halves cut side down on the grill and cook for a few seconds to char.

Slice the pork and serve with the shrimp, oysters, onion, and asparagus, with the charred lemon and lime as a garnish and any remaining sauce in a bowl for dipping.

JAE-YUK BOKKEUM 제육볶음
Gochujang-Marinated Stir-Fried Pork

SERVES 4

13 ounces (360 g) pork shoulder, cut into ¼ by 2-inch (6 mm by 5 cm) slices

⅔ cup (200 g) sauté gochujang (see page 54)

1 large onion, cut into ¾-inch-thick (2 cm) slices

8 to 10 green onions, white parts only, cut diagonally into ¾-inch (2 cm) pieces

8 to 10 garlic cloves, cut into ¼-inch-thick (6 mm) slices

1 Cheongyang chile or jalapeño, thinly sliced

½ teaspoon canola oil

1¼ teaspoons sesame seeds

8 red-leaf lettuce leaves

12 perilla leaves

The symbiotic relationship between gochujang and pork has never been stronger than in this classic, casual, and deeply addictive dish. Stir-fried pork, or jae-yuk bokkeum, accompanied by lettuce leaves to make ssam is Korean soul food. Along with kimchi jjigae, it's what I miss most when I'm traveling abroad. At Mingles, it is by far the favorite staff meal. Since each cook has his or her own personal variation—some are spicier, some come with adventurous additions like perilla leaves and kimchi—the dish is a revealing peek into the chefs' individual tastes and skills. The keys to making this dish are to start with high-quality pork and to find the balance in which the gochujang augments but doesn't obscure the flavor of the meat.

In a bowl, mix together the pork, gochujang, onion, green onions, garlic, and chile. Cover and refrigerate for 30 minutes to 1 hour. (If you let it sit for too long, the gochujang will overwhelm the pork.)

When ready to cook, in a large cast-iron skillet or a wok, heat the canola oil over medium heat until shimmering. Add the pork-vegetable mixture, increase the heat to high, and stir-fry until the pork is browned and cooked through, 8 to 10 minutes.

Sprinkle with the sesame seeds and serve immediately with the lettuce and perilla leaves.

GOCHUJANG PULLED PORK SANDWICH

고추장 풀드 포크 샌드위치

SERVES 4

FOR THE PORK

1½ teaspoons fennel seeds

1½ teaspoons coriander seeds

1½ teaspoons whole black peppercorns

⅓ cup (100 g) BBQ gochujang (see page 55)

1 tablespoon pure maple syrup

1½ teaspoons Cajun seasoning

1½ teaspoons onion powder

1½ teaspoons garlic powder

1½ teaspoons gochugaru

18 ounces (500 g) boneless pork shoulder

1 medium onion, thinly sliced

1 teaspoon hot sauce

1 teaspoon apple cider vinegar

FOR THE AIOLI

6 tablespoons (90 g) mayonnaise

2 tablespoons gochujang

1 tablespoon fresh lemon juice

1 garlic clove, finely chopped

4 hamburger buns, toasted

1 cucumber, thinly sliced lengthwise on a mandoline

This sandwich combines two of the world's most hallowed barbecue traditions: those of South Korea and the American South. Gochujang is pork's greatest friend, and it blends harmoniously with the vinegar sauces of North Carolina barbecue. After a lot of experimentation, I landed on this combination of sweetness and spice, both in the marinade and in the vinegary sauce that gets folded into the pork at the end.

MAKE THE PORK: Using a mortar and pestle or spice grinder, finely grind the fennel, coriander, and peppercorns. In a large bowl, mix together the ground spices, BBQ gochujang, maple syrup, Cajun seasoning, onion powder, garlic powder, and gochugaru. Rub the mixture evenly all over the pork shoulder, cover, and marinate in the refrigerator for at least 6 hours and up to overnight.

Spread the onion in a thin layer across the bottom of an electric pressure rice cooker. Place the marinated pork atop the onion and cook on the slow-cooking mode for 2 hours, until the meat is tender and breaks down easily with a fork. Let cool in the rice cooker, then transfer the meat to a bowl and shred it.

Strain the sauce from the rice cooker into a small pot. Cook over medium heat to reduce the liquid by half, about 5 minutes. Stir the reduced sauce, hot sauce, and vinegar into the shredded meat.

MAKE THE AIOLI: In a small bowl, whisk together the mayonnaise, gochujang, lemon juice, and garlic until incorporated.

To serve, toast the hamburger buns in a toaster oven, then spread 2 tablespoons of the gochujang aioli on the top and bottom of each bun. Divide the pulled pork evenly among the buns, add a few slices of cucumber, and serve immediately.

TIP: If you don't have a pressure rice cooker, use this cast-iron-pot method instead: After marinating the meat, cut the pork into ¾-inch (2 cm) cubes and place them in a large cast-iron pot with a lid. Add the onion and 1¼ cups (300 ml) water and bring to a boil over medium heat. Reduce the heat to low, cover, and braise the pork for 2 hours, stirring every 15 minutes or so, until the meat is tender and breaks down easily with a fork. Remove the meat from the braising liquid and shred it, then return it to the pot and let it simmer slowly until the braising liquid has been absorbed. Mix the meat with the hot sauce and vinegar.

GOCHUJANG CHOCOLATE MOUSSE

고추장 초콜릿 무스

SERVES 4

6 ounces (170 g) dark chocolate, such as Valrhona Caraïbe, cut into chunks

¾ cup (180 ml) heavy cream

2 tablespoons gochujang

1½ teaspoons corn syrup

12 butter cookies

Dark chocolate and spice have always been a perfect combination of bitterness, sweet, and heat. Add the gamchilmat of gochujang, and the result is a dessert as complex in its flavor as it is easy to make. Though this recipe comes from Mingles, I make it at home with my kids all the time. The sharpness of the gochujang combined with the sultry chocolate and the richness of the cream is undeniably, unutterably delicious.

Place the chocolate chunks in a heatproof bowl. Fill a medium pot with water and bring to a boil over medium-low heat. Reduce the heat to low and place the bowl of chocolate on top of the pot; make sure the bottom of the bowl does not touch the water. Use a spatula to stir frequently until the chocolate reaches 113°F (45°C).

Meanwhile, in another pot, combine the cream, gochujang, and corn syrup. Cook over low heat, stirring, until the temperature reaches 122°F (50°C).

Once both the chocolate and the cream mixture have reached the desired temperature, pour half the cream mixture into the bowl with the chocolate and use a whisk to combine. Pour in the remaining cream mixture and whisk until well combined. Using a hand blender, blend until the mixture is fully emulsified (it will be uniform in color), then transfer to a wide glass container with a lid. Cover the surface of the mousse with plastic wrap, seal the container, and refrigerate for 1 to 2 hours, until set.

Just before serving, allow the mousse to come to room temperature. Serve with the butter cookies.

TIP: For a fancy gochujang chocolate cookie sandwich, spread some gochujang chocolate mousse between two cookies and sprinkle gochujang powder on top.

JANGBONGA

Sunchang, a town in Korea's southwest Jeolla Province, is gochujang heaven. Blessed with crystalline rivers, dense forests, and stunning mountain ranges, Sunchang is ideal for making gochujang. Gangcheon Mountain, with its dense forests, protects the town from harsh winter wind. The Seomjin River, fed by underground aquifers, offers pristine water. Here peppers flourish in the heat and humidity while the fluctuations in temperature between night and day are perfect for fermentation.

Though the natural environment undoubtedly has much to do with Sunchang's historical importance to jang making, as with so much of our history, it all goes back to the Joseon dynasty. The dynasty's first king, Taejo, is said to have first tasted Sunchang gochujang at a Buddhist temple in the mountains here, and loved it so much he asked that the jang be sent to the royal court in northern Seoul once he became king. Sunchang gochujang became a staple at the palace, appearing in court records throughout the dynasty's five-century rule. By the twentieth century, its place atop the jang hierarchy was cemented.

Today Sunchang is a small town where gochujang looms large. Beginning with the construction of the 88 Olympic Expressway, a highway built for the 1988 Summer Olympics that connects Gwangju and Daegu, Sunchang's gochujang has spread across the country. In the early 1990s, the Korean government spent $11 million to create Gochujang Village, both as a tourist destination and as a way to protect this bastion of tradition.

The main road of Gochujang Village, Minsokmaeul-gil, is a long sloping one that starts in the belly of a valley and ends in the foothills of Gangcheonsan. At the base of the road is the Sunchang Jang Museum, 16,000 square feet (1,500 sq m) full of dioramas of gochujang artisans, historic tools, and helpful displays. Its upper end terminates in a small park where cartoon figures of jangdok, peppers, and meju cavort among landscaped bushes near a waterwheel. There is a gochujang experience center where children and tourist groups experiment with making their own jang, and many souvenir shops. Each side of the road within the village is lined with hanok, traditional Korean houses, occupied with gochujang makers. In courtyards with imposing gates topped with peaked tiled roofs, fields of jangdok, filled with gochujang, age.

There are forty-two gochujang makers in Gochujang Village, but only one master artisan. Her name is Kang Soon-Ok. Her image—lips painted red, black hair up, wearing a silken hanbok (traditional Korean dress)—smiles down from numerous signs hanging above and around her shop. Framed medals and prizes are proudly displayed. As befits a heavily touristed stretch, Soon-Ok regularly entertains visitors with a make-your-own-gochujang workshop that takes place in a large tiled room adjacent to her shop. But it's more than just a showroom. The back half of the space, cordoned off with string, is occupied by jangdok. Each jangdok is ringed in heavy rope, with charcoal, balls of cotton, and bright red dried peppers around its neck. The decorated chimneys of two gamasot are etched with adorable facial features. Meju, strung in rice straw, hang from wooden latticework. Though these tools are largely decorative, as the boxes and boxes of product that share the space attest, Soon-Ok's is a flourishing productive business.

When she emerges from behind the jangdok wearing the same silken robes as those seen on the signs (she changes for visitors), Soon-Ok moves with the quickness and impatience of a much younger person. She's all business. In her seventies now, Soon-Ok was born and grew up in Sunchang. She comes from a long line of gochujang artisans, but as she tells us, when she was growing up, her family made gochujang only for themselves.

Like many in Korea, and even more so in these rural regions, Soon-Ok's life was transformed by the 6-2-5 War, which impoverished the countryside. To make her story even more tragic, when she was just four, her father passed away. He was thirty-seven. That left Soon-Ok, her mother, and her older brother and sisters to fend for themselves. Options for a poor, fatherless young girl in rural Korea in the 1950s were limited, to say the least. Though Soon-Ok excelled in school, she dropped out after elementary school to help her mother at home. She would venture into the mountains to harvest wood for fuel for the gamasot, forage for herbs like dureup and minari for cooking, and lug home glutinous rice, soybeans, and, of course, gochu from nearby farms. She'd come back weighted down with her prodigious bounty. "I was always very ambitious," she says. "I wanted to be the leader of all the ladies in town. I constantly thought about how I could become the best and be better than others. Even nowadays, I think about this every day."

Back at home, Soon-Ok and her mother made gochujang in the traditional way. Rinsing the rice carefully, then boiling it; rinsing the soybeans and boiling them; combining the two and forming them with a ratio of six parts rice to four parts soybeans into meju. They began making the meju in August and finished the gochujang in October. The making of gochujang is a more active process than the making of ganjang or doenjang. It involves not only methodically grinding the meju and the sun-dried gochu but also laboriously stirring the mixture as it heats, then letting it cool, gently, to foster microbial growth. Even as a young girl, Soon-Ok took on the brunt of the work. "My mother was thirty-two with four children," she explained. "I tried to do as much for her as I could."

Eventually Soon-Ok married the son of a professional gochujang artisan. She was quickly initiated into her husband's family's business. When her sister-in-law moved to Seoul, Soon-Ok stepped in more fully and applied for a license to make gochujang in 1979. This became the first step on her path toward becoming a gochujang artisan. One reason gochujang—and jang making in general—is flourishing today is a concerted effort by the Korean Ministry of Agriculture, Food and Rural Affairs to safeguard and promote traditional foodways. It isn't easy. To become an artisan, the highest rank, one must have lived in Sunchang for twenty-five years and demonstrated excellence through winning myriad awards and prizes.

Soon-Ok was named a gochujang master artisan by the government in 2015. One reason Jangbonga's gochujang is considered among the best in Sunchang, and therefore the best in Korea, is precisely the same ambition that compelled Soon-Ok, as a young

girl, to outgather the others in the village. "I demand the highest-quality ingredients," she says: sun-dried gochu bright in color and flavor, the highest-quality rice from local farmers, the highest-quality soybeans from her producers. Though she makes between 22 and 33 tons (20 to 30 metric tons) of gochujang a year, nothing in her process has changed, she says.

Soon-Ok continues to learn. The jangdok that surround her aren't full of gochujang for sale. Rather, they contain all sorts of other experiments: doenjang from 2009, gochujang from 1991. Inside one is an inky-black paste, used for medicine more than cuisine. They symbolize Soon-Ok's relentless pursuit of knowledge. "I'm an artisan," she explains. "I need to know everything about jang."

RESOURCES

Markets
H Mart
Hmart.com

Wooltari
Wooltariusa.com

Kim'C Market
Kimcmarket.com

Jangs
Yangjo ganjang recommendations:
Sempio 501
Sempio 701

Hansik ganjang recommendations:
Mcgguroom Golden Joseon Ganjang
Baekmalsoon Traditional Ganjang
Kisoondo Traditional Ganjang
Sempio Chosun Ganjang for Soup
Jookjangyeon Premium Ganjang

Yangjo doenjang recommendations:
CJ Haechandle Soybean Paste, Korean
    Doenjang
Chung Jung One Sunchang Doenjang

Hansik doenjang recommendations:
Mcgguroom Golden Mac Doenjang
Jookjangyeon Premium Doenjang
Kisoondo Traditional Doenjang
Baekmalsoon Korean Traditional Doenjang

Artisan gochujang recommendations:
Sunchang Moon Ok-Rye Traditional
    Gochujang
Jangbonga Gochujang
Mcgguroom Glutinous Gochujang
Jookjangyeon Premium Gochujang
Kisoondo Traditional Gochujang

Commercial gochujang recommendations:
CJ Haechandle Traditional Gochujang
    (mild, hot)
Chung Jung One O'Food Traditional
    Sunchang Gochujang
Sempio Organic Gochujang
Sempio Vegan Gochujang

ACKNOWLEDGMENTS

MINGOO KANG

Thank you to Joshua, a co-author who learned to understand Korean cuisine deeply; we studied together and he conveyed my cooking beautifully in English. And to Nadia, a co-author who made my vague dream of creating a book that introduces Korean cuisine come true. Thank you as well to Judy Pray and the entire team at Artisan for helping shepherd this book into being.

Thanks to Nayoung and Junsu, two precious people who have been with me for every part of the process of making this book. Also to Team Mingles, Mama Lee, and Hansik Goo, who supported this project in so many ways.

Thank you to chef Cho Hee-Sook and Buddhist nun Jeong Kwan, who teach me lifelong lessons beyond cooking. Photographer Dong-gil Yun and food stylist Ayeon Lee poured all their passion into this project, too.

Thanks to director Park Hong-In and CEO Lee Sung-Gon of *Bar & Dining* magazine; Professor Jeong Hye-Kyeong, who taught so much so I could deliver accurate information about jangs; Sempio Company; and all the jang masters who helped us.

Thank you to my beloved family: Dohee, Dain, Yunhoo, my father, my younger brother Shingu, my mother, my mother-in-law, and my father-in-law.

And finally, I would like to give thanks and share this book with all the chef friends around the world who always support me.

JOSHUA DAVID STEIN

I'd like to thank everyone who helped put this book together, and there are many people. Obviously, I'd like to thank Chef Mingoo Kang for his dedication, expertise, and vision and Nadia Cho for her passion and savvy. This book couldn't have happened without the work of Nayoung Kim, who worked tirelessly as guide, translator, problem-solver, factotum, taster, tester, and friend; and Junsu Shin, who doggedly refined the recipes you'll find here during all hours of the day and night. Irene Yoo, our recipe tester, went above and beyond in every single aspect of this process, and I owe her a deep debt of gratitude. Dong-gil, our dogged photographer, shot and reshot over the course of two years, always cheerful, always professional, and always excellent. Thanks to Matt Rodbard for clueing me in to the magic of jang in general and this project in particular, and to David Black, my agent, for helping this book get across the finish line. A huge thanks to the Artisan team, starting with Judy Pray, the kindest editor a writer could hope for, and to Ivy McFadden, our punctilious copy editor. A cookbook is only as good as it's grammar.

NADIA CHO

I would like to acknowledge the chefs, journalists, and directors I have worked with since I began the journey to promote Korean food in the United States back in 2008.

Chef Mingoo Kang and Joshua David Stein, I am so grateful and lucky to have gone on this long adventure with you. You both have been the best co-authors and also my most trustworthy companions for the last four years.

I can't thank the team enough: Nayoung, who has been dedicated to this book from the beginning; Junsu, who supported the recipes; Dong-gil, the photographer who made our recipes and the stories come alive; and Ayeon, the stylist who guided us with her expertise.

Thank you, Mom and Dad. Dad, I know you are always watching me from heaven, and Mom, thank you for teaching me the beauty of Korean food.

Thank you, Jay, my son. You are my motivation for pushing to contribute to Korean culture.

Thank you, Chef Eric Ripert, for contributing your foreword to the book, and Matt Rodbard, for encouraging me to write this book.

Thank you, Angela Miller, for all your support, and Judy Pray, our editor at Artisan, for your trust.

I give my thanks to all the jang masters who shared their experience with us.

INDEX

Page numbers in *italics* refer to photos.

Dong-gil Yun

MINGOO KANG is the chef and owner of Mingles, located in Seoul, which has been named one of Asia's 50 Best Restaurants and holds two Michelin stars. Kang's approach at Mingles of presenting innovative hansik has earned him both domestic and international acclaim, and he frequently collaborates with chefs around the world. Most recently, in 2021, he was awarded the Inedit Damm Chefs' Choice Award—the only accolade voted for by the other chefs on the Asia's 50 Best Restaurants list. In addition to Mingles, Chef Kang runs a retail market in Seoul called MamaLee Market; Hansik Goo, which offers creative Korean cuisine in Hong Kong; and the popular fried chicken brand Hyodo Chicken.

DeSean McClinton-Holland

JOSHUA DAVID STEIN is a writer based in New York City. He is the author of *Cooking for Your Kids: At Home with the World's Greatest Chefs* and the coauthor of *Notes from a Young Black Chef* and *My America: Recipes from a Young Black Chef*, both with Kwame Onwuachi; *The Nom Wah Cookbook*, with Wilson Tang; *Il Buco: Stories and Recipes*, with Donna Lennard; *Vino: An Essential Guide to Real Italian Wine*, with Joe Campanale; and *Food & Beer*, with Jeppe Jarnit-Bjergsø and Daniel Burns. He is also the author of *To Me He Was Just Dad: Stories of Growing Up with Famous Fathers* and a number of award-winning children's books, including *Can I Eat That?*, *What's Cooking?*, and *Solitary Animals*.

Diane Kang

NADIA CHO is the founder of Jeong Culture and Communication, which is dedicated to promoting Korean food in the United States. She has been a liaison for chefs and journalists to Korean food and has worked with *Bon Appétit*, *Condé Nast Traveler*, *Food & Wine*, and the *New York Times* and *T Magazine* to bring chefs and journalists to Korea. She was the producer of the "Jeong Kwan" episode of *Chef's Table* and helped produce episodes for *Anthony Bourdain: Parts Unknown* and other shows on the Cooking Channel, NBC, ABC, and many others. She has produced and directed Korean food content on Eater.com.